# BRITISH GAME SHOOTING

*To my mother and father*
*for their encouragement*

# BRITISH
# GAME
# SHOOTING
## ROUGHSHOOTING AND WILDFOWLING

# BRIAN P MARTIN

WARD LOCK LIMITED · LONDON

*ACKNOWLEDGEMENTS*
The author and publishers would like to thank the following people
and organizations for their help in supplying photographs for this
book: Terry Andrewartha/Survival Anglia p 81; Dr Alan Beaumont
p 108; Gordon Carlisle p 145; Mark Cator/Impact p 29;
D. N. Dalton/NHPA p 153; Manfred Danegger/NHPA p 111;
John Darling pp 17, 57, 124-5; Dennis Green/Survival Anglia p 92;
David Grewcock pp 12-13, 33, 37, 40, 61, 128, 136, 141;
Ray Kennedy p 89; John Marchington Photo Library pp 20-1, 48,
121, 133, 148, 156; Hans Reinhard/Bruce Coleman Ltd pp 64-5, 72;
Roy Shaw p 165; Arthur Shepherd p 117;
Michael Strobino/Survival Anglia p 84.

Text © Brian P. Martin 1988
Colour illustrations © Ward Lock 1988

First published in Great Britain in 1988
by Ward Lock Limited, 8 Clifford Street
London W1X 1RB, an Egmont Company

Editor Richard Dawes
Designed by Ann Thompson
Colour illustrations by David Hurrell
Text filmset in 11/13pt Caslon 540
by Dorchester Typesetting Group Ltd
Printed and bound in Italy by
Canale

British Library Cataloguing in Publication Data

Martin, Brian P. (Brian Philip), 1947-
British gameshooting.
1. Great Britain. Game annuals. Shooting
I. Title
799.2′13′0941

ISBN 0-7063-6685-9

# CONTENTS

# PREFACE

Shooting sports, such as gameshooting, pigeon shooting and wildfowling, have become very popular in recent years. Almost a million people from all walks of life are involved, and class and social backgrounds are no longer seen as barriers. Shooting has become the sport of everyone who enjoys remote countryside and who has the initiative to find a way of getting into it and sufficient leisure and funds.

*British Gameshooting* covers all the important shotgun shooting sports involving live quarry in a sensitive and informative way. Brian Martin introduces both the novice and the seasoned Gun to the joys, social niceties and legal requirements of all the different types of quarry shooting available in Britain today. He discusses each quarry species in great detail, from the elusive ptarmigan and capercaillie to the more common woodpigeon and mallard, providing insight into their natural habitats and breeding cycles to inspire a real love of the natural history in the reader.

It is particularly apposite that a book of this kind should appear when the shooting community is coming increasingly under public scrutiny. The menace of tight legal controls, possibly including compulsory examinations, can only be combatted by following the codes of practice and safety procedures advocated by the BASC and outlined clearly in this book. Only in this way can shooting continue to benefit sportsmen, and contribute to the conservation of so much of our natural heritage.

John Swift
The British Association
for Shooting & Conservation

# INTRODUCTION

In this enlightened age of conservation, when 'big game' shooting for sport alone is wriggling in its death throes, it matters not that Britain has no elephants or tigers. Neither do we have much 'middle game', such as the wild boar which increasingly attract adventurous western sportsmen to rough, unsophisticated countries such as Tunisia and Pakistan. We do offer a good range of deerstalking, which is a significant foreign currency earner, but it is in 'small game', chiefly birds, that the great strength of British shooting lies today, and that is the nucleus of this book.

*Previous pages* Beaters on the way to the next drive: for most simply being there is enough.

I am not so much preoccupied with recording every single technical and organizational detail enabling the hunter to achieve his bag, for there is a wealth of specialist titles which cover this adequately. What I am mostly concerned with is the social side of shooting, such as good sportsmanship and etiquette, and describing all the excitement and atmosphere which makes British gameshooting the envy of the modern world.

Thus we will range from the ritualized social scene of the formal pheasant shoot to solo pot-hunting for a modest mixed bag, from high-tops ptarmigan to lowland pigeon decoying, from the thrill of the grouse moor and partridge manor to coastal wildfowling after duck and geese—as close as we'll ever get to wilderness hunting in Britain.

Almost a million people shoot game (in its widest sense) in Britain today—more than at any other time in our history—and the number is growing steadily in line with increasing prosperity and leisure time. If this vast army of hunters wandered at will without regard for property, privacy, and the safety of others, as well as the continued well-being of our countryside and wildlife, obviously chaos would ensue in such a densely populated island. Thus, whatever branch of the sport we choose to follow we must adhere strictly to both legislation and unwritten codes of conduct and support those national organizations which champion a sensible and practical attitude to shooting.

Yet the most expensive sport is not necessarily the most satisfying. Indeed, some of our richest countrymen take more delight in a solo walkabout for quarry such as pigeon, duck, and snipe than in the refinements of even their biggest and best driven days. They find that the greatest and most lasting rewards come through a close knowledge of nature, the coast and countryside, and the quarry, which is a perfect complement to the traditional thrill of the chase.

Many sportsmen delight in hunting a variety of quarry, which takes them to a wide range of wild places throughout varied seasons. This, fortuitously, enables those with the time and money to savour the best of each season and enjoy a very full autumn and winter.

The action really begins in late July, when combines advance on the cornfields, immediately attracting concentrations of woodpigeons, which gobble up the spilt grain, providing superb sport for the decoyer. But there is no close season for this great agricultural pest and excellent opportunities to shoot it will arise at other times of year.

The first game season proper begins on 12 August—the famous 'Glorious Twelfth', when sportsmen of the world gather on the grouse moors of northern Britain to test their skills against what many regard as the king of gamebirds. But the number and timing of grouse days will vary greatly with the season, for this is a truly wild quarry, subject to many pressures such as cyclical disease, and none are reared and released. Good habitat management is the key to successful grouse shooting.

But in an average year our privileged sportsman will shoot most of his grouse in August, perhaps returning for later 'mopping-up' days when late-developing birds are more wary and stronger on the wing. From 1 September his attention will focus on partridge and wildfowl, but with both the cream of the sport is to come later. If he is lucky he will have a shootable surplus of the declining grey or English partridge on his ground, but most Guns now rely on the introduced redlegged or French partridge for sport. Both will be at their best from October, when their pinions are strong and they have been driven a few times.

September wildfowl are also of lesser interest, except for the duck which provide good sport on inland stubbles. The best duck, goose, and wader shooting will begin in November and continue right through to 20 February on the coast of mainland Britain, for there is nothing the wildfowler likes better than strong winds, battling weather, and dawn and dusk flights after the wealth of migrants which winter here.

Pheasant shooting begins in colourful October, when it really does feel as if the land is primed ready to deliver its natural harvest, of which our game is such an important part.

But while there are good, seasoned pheasants to be bagged in October, most birds will be of the year and many shoots will spare them for November, when they are far stronger on the wing and most of the leaf will be off the trees.

After November's mighty climax, when the great woods echo to main pheasant days, we descend gently through December's pleasant brew of mixed and modest days laced with well-chosen excursions after other quarry. There will be ample opportunity to seek out the cold-loving ptarmigan before winter seals off his Highland penthouse, the elusive snipe in lowland bog and marsh, the black grouse on his rough, northern hills, and the revered and mystical woodcock, all before the great traditional explosion of Boxing Day.

January brings 'cocks only' days to many pheasant shoots, but what superb sport with wily longtails examining the best of us, often in teeth-rattling weather. But then the hardy wildfowler is truly in his element and will study the ways of wind and tide to station himself beneath wigeon and whitefront, pintail and pinkfoot, and all those other visitors from the north which epitomize the hunter's wilderness.

All the gameshooting seasons end on or before 1 February, but even then there is plenty to entertain. Pigeon roosts have built up throughout the winter in the big woods, and with February and March comes the opportunity to shoot them at dusk without disturbing the pheasants and before the birds disperse for another breeding season.

Foreshore wildfowling continues up to 20 February and later still there is plenty of rabbit and hare shooting as well as further pigeon shooting on crops such as peas and greens. In fact there is hardly time to catch our breath and lay plans before July is with us, pheasant poults are put to wood and the gameshooter's year has turned full circle again.

Today we have just thirty-three bird species of significant sporting interest. A few are classified as 'pests' but most are also shot for the pot and the majority of Guns will shoot only that which they can eat. But in olden times, when there was little concept of conservation and subsistence shooting was more important, a very wide range of species, ranging from larks to swans, ended up in every market. However, many songbirds continue to be shot overseas, even in advanced countries such as France and Italy, where there is traditionally greater interest in wild foods.

In Britain the most recent significant legislation came in 1981, when the Wildlife and Countryside Act removed thirteen species from the quarry list. Voices are still raised in some quarters over the protection of curlew (except in Northern Ireland) and redshank, two waders which remain very common.

However, there has been increasingly close co-operation between shooting and conservation interests and, despite the determined efforts of minority anti groups, today's quarry list seems secure. And there is every chance that one or two species will be gained. In 1987 the Canada goose, already shot elsewhere in the UK, was added to the Northern Ireland list as it was becoming such a pest there, while brent goose numbers continue to grow so rapidly that it cannot be too long before they are reinstated as legal quarry in England at least.

Game laws were enacted long before guns were commonly used in the field. Deer and hare were then of chief interest and the longbow, hawk and hound were employed by the privileged few, primarily those with property, for the hunt. Not surprisingly, in days when poverty and starvation were commonplace this was the source of great friction and poaching was rife. Cruel penalties were introduced, with gaol for many offences and even transportation and hanging in the most serious cases. And game preserves were littered with hideous man traps with toothed jaws to grab and maim the unwary. But despite all this there were many poor folk prepared to risk all, to creep up the hedgerows in search of 'one for the pot' for their very large families. The incentive was great. In the early nineteenth century, for example, a pheasant would sell for the equivalent of five days' wages for a labourer.

Though gunpowder was certainly used in England in the thirteenth century, it is thought that guns were not fired at birds in Europe before the fifteenth century. Early weapons were very unreliable and cumbersome and it was not until well into the eighteenth century that they were efficient enough to attract the sporting gentry.

The big breakthrough came in the 1850s with the first reliable breechloaders, firing ready-made cartridges, providing the rapid

firepower which would stimulate demand for big bags. The 12-bore became the most popular gun and after the 1870s hammerless models steadily took over. Later improvements to increase speed of firing were the cartridge-ejecting mechanism and single trigger to fire both barrels, though even today many guns do without them. In fact the standard British game gun remains much as it was in the late nineteenth century.

For partridges in numbers like this the driven shooter really needs a cartridge-ejecting gun and help with loading.

At the same time as sporting guns were being perfected, access to wild places became much easier through the extension of the railways, road improvement, and the introduction of the motor car. This greatly increased the demand for shooting and as southern rents shot up more northerly ground was eagerly sought. Today, with high-speed transport at our disposal, all land worth shooting is in big demand. The affluent London businessman thinks nothing of using his helicopter to visit his northern moor, while Americans arriving on Concorde to shoot British pheasants are an everyday occurrence.

Rapid and cheap transport has also made its mark at the low-cost end of shooting. Today's wildfowler must be highly mobile to take advantage of favourable weather and to reach his destination at very unsocial hours when no public transport is running, especially to out-of-the-way places. The pigeon shooter too must be very independent, ready to go when the big flocks descend on the crops he is supposed to be protecting and able to reach places far from public transport.

Before the advent of easy travel, the few gentleman sport shooters had to travel by coach or even horseback for days on end, often along bumpy, pot-holed tracks. Only the adventurous went to wild, out-of-the-way places such as Scotland in search of grouse, ptarmigan, and the like.

Then there were in most areas market gunners who were concerned with the certainty of killing rather than sport. They often used nets, decoys, nooses, and other traps to catch fowl, and when the Gun came along they had no qualms over bagging sitters. Large bores, including puntguns, became common as they were capable of killing many birds with one shot.

Shooting at flying birds began in the first half of the seventeenth century and was well established by 1800. Early Sports pottered about the woods and fields with their dogs to flush game—perhaps with a few friends and a keeper or two in attendance. With this walking-up method bags were inevitably small, but what fine exercise it provided and what joy there must have been in wandering about countryside which was still very much as nature intended. It is not surprising then that in these days of overcrowded, high-pressure living there is a distinct resurgence of interest in walked-up shooting.

For this more solitary sport the ideal gamebird was the native English partridge, so common in the last century, when its coveys were the delight of countrymen throughout the land. Sadly, its decline began early with the introduction of intensive farming, ploughing-up of heaths and commons, drainage, and general tidying-up of the countryside as well as the use of poisonous chemicals on the land. Yet it was still shot in large numbers until about 1950.

It was the more easily managed pheasant which became the focus of attention in the second half of the nineteenth century and the introduction of intensive rearing and release facilitated the big bags around which the great shooting parties revolved. Everywhere the rich and famous gathered for glittering weekends and while the ladies sparkled at dinner parties the men strove to be top Gun in the firing line. And to support them were vast armies of retainers: keepers, beaters, loaders, dogmen, cartridge-boys, and so on, most living in tied cottages on pittance wages in an extension of medieval serfdom.

The collapse of this system really began with World War I, when every man demanded a better standard of living and inheritance taxation started to break up the great estates. There was ample opportunity for the *nouveaux riches* of the rising middle class to buy into shoots, thus relieving owners of much financial burden. Others got together in small groups to rent parcels of land, employ gamekeepers and form the syndicates which today are the backbone of British gameshooting. But now the emphasis has rightly shifted from size of bag to quality of sport.

More recently, as costs have escalated, the do-it-yourself shoot has taken off and this really has allowed men of modest means to enjoy the hitherto generally exclusive sport of driven gameshooting. In this there is no professional gamekeeper and the Guns themselves provide the labour: often one or two of the more enthusiastic ones will do the bulk of the rearing and release in return for free shooting. And the others will have relatively cheap sport as well.

Also this decade we have witnessed the rise of commercialism, which, as we will see, has its bad as well as good aspects. Guns can buy, largely through sporting agents, shooting by the day, week, or longer and can even choose a certain bag, paying so much per bird. It is a 'made-to-measure' service which goes hand-in-hand with the new drive for diversification in land use, but it certainly has its opponents among traditionalists.

In complete contrast is wildfowling, a very cheap sport, but its nationwide system of clubs ensures the very highest standards of conduct and there is little point in taking up this arduous activity unless you are both physically fit and dedicated. But should you succeed, the rewards are great: the pursuit of truly wild, migratory birds through all weathers in the wildest and most beautiful places does wonders for the soul.

Even more popular today is woodpigeon shooting as it can often be obtained completely free, providing the farmer with an important pest-control service. Indeed, this is the only bird which many ever shoot. Yet pigeon shooting is a relatively young sport as it was only in this century that the bird became extremely common. It was originally a species of the deciduous forest and remained in modest numbers until farming provided vast acreages of new foods, especially crops which stand through the lean months of midwinter.

All our other quarry species are doing well too and none is in the least way endangered, as we shall see in subsequent chapters. Together they provide endless opportunities for folk from every walk of life to satisfy the important and ancient hunting instinct, and are the means through which so many people keep in touch with nature and really appreciate the rhythm of the seasons.

So many of our sportsmen are also devoted conservationists and provide both valuable practical support and observations and statistics for our research biologists and countryside managers. And both directly and indirectly they provide huge amounts of money and vast acreages for the benefit of all our animal and plant life as well as enhancing the landscape. Gameshooters have long been in our front-line defence against the wholesale habitat destruction which threatens the whole fragile fabric of life on earth.

British gameshooting is undeniably in the ascendant. Much of the impetus is derived from the general increase in leisure time and improving standards of living as well as a revival of the economy. The unseen power which constantly pulls us back to our roots in the land and permits peaceful harmony with the great outdoors allows gameshooting to remain socially acceptable in an age when pot-hunting is unnecessary. British gameshooting is certainly here to stay.

# TAKING UP SHOOTING

Shooting is no longer the exclusive sport it once was and anyone with a reasonable amount of patience and courtesy will be welcome to take part irrespective of wealth. Few sports embrace such a friendly community, brought together from all walks of life by a deep-rooted desire to share the excitement of the field. But the enthusiast must be prepared to put back into the sport at least as much as he takes out for he is dealing with a vulnerable and variable harvest.

The lucky ones among us will have been brought up in traditionally sporting families and have had the benefit of fatherly example from an early age. But even this requires care for, as in any activity, the youngster can be turned off by too much of a good thing—a simple case of familiarity breeding contempt. There is also the danger of picking up bad habits but in most cases only good will come through sheltering under the paternal wing and the student will have the great advantage of being able to share his father's established shooting.

The young Gun without fatherly guidance must find his own way. Frequently this will be through a friend or acquaintance, and then the main risk will be demanding too much of that person's time and, of course, his personal shooting. Yet such a chance outing with a chum can often lead to a lifelong passion for shooting.

# FINDING SHOOTING

If you are introduced to shooting through family or friends then obviously you will begin with the type of shooting they already enjoy and perhaps hope to branch out later on. But if you start without contacts you must decide which sort of shooting you want to try and then adopt the particular approach required in order to secure it.

## ROUGHSHOOTING

Very many people start with a small roughshoot—one where there is probably a good range of wild quarry but no rearing and release, no formal driven shoots with high overheads, and the accent is on walked-up shooting, perhaps with a friend or two. This could range from a few acres to entire estates where no formal shooting exists.

Getting such sport was once very easy, especially for those living in the country, but today most landowners are quick to exploit all possible sources of income, no matter how small. Yet it is still possible to get good shooting for virtually nothing, though, of course, it is customary to present one's host with a bottle or two at Christmas and the occasional brace of game. And in this case it really is the thought rather than the quantity that counts. Also it is wise to keep in with the farm manager as well as the owner.

If you don't happen to know any farmers or landowners then you must do your homework. Study the neighbourhood well and if you spot any promising territory which does not appear to be shot, then simply ask for permission. A visit is better than a telephone call because it is harder for the farmer to say no to your face and he will be suspicious of anyone he cannot see. However, if he does turn you down it is worthwhile leaving your telephone number as he may change his mind.

You will be very lucky indeed if you succeed first visit: many people try dozens of farms without success. And be a little wary of the exceptionally generous man as he may have already given permission to other people, as a result of which the shooting could be very poor indeed.

Remember to consider ground other than farmland as there are many rewarding shoots at odd sites such as commercial nurseries, golf courses, private woodlands, gravel workings, and quarries. However, the more unusual the site the greater the restrictions are likely to be.

Once you are accepted you cannot assume that the shooting is yours in perpetuity, so keep looking for further opportunities, perhaps on neighbouring estates to make your patch bigger. The owner can change his mind at any time for a whole variety of reasons, including the possibility of substantial income from someone else after you have shown him the land's potential. He might also justifiably turn you out if you have shot certain quarry which he asked you not to touch, ventured onto forbidden territory, trampled or damaged crops, left your cartridge cases lying about, continually left gates open, frightened his animals, taken along friends to shoot without asking him first, let your dog run riot, been rude to his staff, or not complied with any other express requirement.

You might be able to secure a written agreement, ideally in return for a nominal rent, but this does not give you licence to do as you please and it will probably be renewable annually.

If you are willing to pay a substantial sum for your shoot, perhaps along with a group of friends in a syndicate, then the easiest thing to do is study the regular advertisements in the shooting magazines. Then, almost certainly, you will have to sign an agreement with a minimum period of notice on either side, but do check out the land's potential before committing yourself. Don't put too much store by bag records from seasons past as the ground might have been drastically altered of late. Hedges might have been ripped out, woods felled, fields drained, and severe spraying programmes introduced—just some of the things which will make the place less hospitable to quarry. And always ask yourself why the shoot is available now if it is supposed to be so good.

The best land will have a wide variety of habitats with plenty of thick, natural cover for nesting, trees for roosting, hedgerows for creeping along out of sight of predators, open areas for feeding and basking, marshes for waders and wildfowl, a good supply of natural animal and plant foods, protection from the worst cold, suitable position to attract migratory birds, and little disturbance by man, and will be surrounded by peaceful countryside.

As you win the landowner's confidence you might be able to persuade him to let you create a few clearings where the cover is too thick, plant trees and shrubs for cover and food where vegetation is scant, clear overgrown ponds, or even create new waters. In return, as the shoot improves you could offer to help him in some way or perhaps invite him to shoot with you.

## *DRIVEN GAMESHOOTING*

If you aspire to shoot driven game, involving beaters forcing birds to fly over strategically placed standing Guns, then you must be prepared to pay for the necessary labour, ground rent, and provision of birds in sufficient quantity. But there are now many ways in which you can participate and the expense varies enormously.

Since the decline of the grey partridge, the pheasant has become the focus of British gameshooting, though the former is still driven in many areas. Along with the introduced and more easily managed French or redlegged partridge, the pheasant and grey partridge are reared and released in very large numbers to compensate for the overall destruction and degradation of habitat. Yet there are estates which still produce good bags of entirely wild birds through a careful regime of sympathetic farming and good habitat control.

The famous red grouse of northern moors is also driven in large numbers, but is not reared at all as it will not adapt well to its predominantly heather diet when released. Grouse moors rely on very strict habitat management, especially through systematic heather burning to provide both young shoots for food and longer growth for nesting and hiding in.

Other birds are driven in much smaller numbers and only very locally. These include the black grouse, which occurs in small numbers on high, rough ground in northern Britain. Then there is the huge capercaillie, our largest gamebird, which is confined to the Scottish forests. The woodcock is often shot on pheasant drives throughout Britain, but only in Ireland and a few areas of western Britain do 'cock still concentrate in sufficient numbers to make driving worthwhile. The same is true of the common snipe, though both species are still extensively walked-up.

Driven gameshooting has evolved over the last century or so into a highly organized social sport and there is little point in getting into it if you don't enjoy the company of other Guns.

If you want your own regular shoot you might be lucky enough to persuade a landowner to let you and your friends develop a driven shoot on his ground free of charge, but most good driving country is already exploited. If you do manage it then make sure that you invite the landowner and/or his farm manager to join in the shooting regularly so that he maintains an active interest and will be more inclined to listen to your special requests, such as permission to plant game crops or create woodland rides.

Most shooting rights are avidly sought after and before you enter the open market you must sort out with your syndicate of fellow Guns just how much you are prepared to pay. Do you want to employ a professional gamekeeper or will lack of finance force you into a do-it-yourself shoot? These are just two of the important questions which soon make you realize that it is best to join a syndicate of Guns with a roughly similar standard of living and with whom you are likely to get on. The nucleus of a successful syndicate is often a group of old friends or family, but others are bold enough to advertise for complete strangers to join them. However, taking on land individually before securing the support of other Guns is very risky.

Once your syndicate is formed, you could place your own 'shoot wanted' advert in the sporting and farming journals, and certainly study all the adverts for sporting rights to let, to give you an idea of what to pay. You will also see 'Guns wanted' adverts where syndicates want to replace members who have dropped out.

Sporting agents may also be approached and could well provide guidance where initial rents need to be established, as could the Game Conservancy. But no matter how gentlemanly the landowner, get your agreement down on paper, if necessary after consulting an experienced solicitor. Nominate a syndicate captain to sign documents and record details such as the names of the lessee and lessor, the precise area of land involved (ideally marked on a map), prohibited zones, special restrictions and length of lease (normally sporting rights are let from 2 February for annual periods, but for seven-year terms). Long leases will also benefit the landowner in that improvements by the lessee will increase the estate's sporting value.

Length of notice required by either party to terminate the agreement should be stated, and just in case there is a major disagreement early on, there should be break clauses after one and three years. In days of high inflation it is better to have an index-linked rental rather than the traditional biennial or triennial review by negotiation.

In England and Wales there are also sporting rates, which normally fall on the lessee and are levied if shooter and farmer are different parties. But in Scotland sporting rates are applicable to all regardless.

The agreement should also make clear who else has access to the land, where public roads, footpaths and bridleways are, who is responsible for pest control, who has the deerstalking rights, whether foxhunts are allowed access, and how many foxes may be shot. The landowner or farmer may wish to retain the right for himself or a friend to roughshoot over all or part of the property or to retain a gun or guns in the syndicate itself. These last two conditions would be compensated for by a reduction in rent, but it is sensible to clarify what bag would be expected and when in the season it would be required.

Many other special conditions are often required by either party. For example, the lessor may restrict shooting to certain times and certain levels, forbid shooting of less common species and insist on insurance cover against damage to farm animals or crops. The lessee may secure the right to grow special game food or cover crops in certain places, to be notified in advance of significant crop or stock changes and to sub-let part of the shoot or certain days. Clarification of as many points as possible will pave the way for a sound, long-lasting relationship, yet a reasonable and flexible approach should always be maintained.

In the DIY shoot sport is more geared to what Guns can afford once the rent has been met. Costs can be cut by having a relatively large team of Guns—say sixteen to twenty instead of the usual seven or eight, who form two teams, each beating on alternate drives.

Bags need only be modest, with the emphasis on good habitat management and wild birds rather than game-farm stock or undertaking a comprehensive rearing and release programme.

Predator control can be given special attention in the old-fashioned labour-intensive way so that every valuable bird put down has an increased chance of survival to the shooting season. Some Guns might have access to cheap or even free grain for feed, while others can put skills such as carpentry and engineering to good use in making release pens and rearing units or maintaining shoot vehicles.

Paid pickers-up are unnecessary as most of the Guns will have their own dogs and be glad to run them. Neither is there need for an expensive lunch—sandwiches and soup in the barn will suffice.

Determination and hard work can bring many economies and if the emphasis is on presenting quality birds—high, wide and handsome—then every one will be worth ten of the squire's 'floppers' from up the road. Much time and effort may be saved by paying for one of the excellent Game Conservancy's advisory visits or attending one of their keepering courses or game management days.

But today there is no need to have your own shoot at all. Like it or not, commercialism has really taken off in the 1980s and any type of shooting can now be bought. In fact, costs have risen so rapidly that very few big shoots today are entirely private in the sense that the owner alone pays for everything.

Grouse moors were let way back in the nineteenth century, but it was after World War I that many great estate owners felt the pinch so much that they were forced to invite friends to share the costs in return for a few days' driven sport at grouse, pheasant, and partridge. This was the beginning of commercialism, for many owners soon tired of the whole thing and let the sporting rights over their entire estates to individuals who formed their own syndicates. Others soon realized that even more money was to be made through letting single days to individuals or companies who would form their own parties as they did not have their own permanent shoots on which to entertain and reciprocate invitations. Today this is very big business indeed and there is particular growth in company days on 'famous name' shoots, often with food and accommodation in palatial surroundings.

But individuals can also buy more modest let driven days for single Guns, often through one of the many sporting hotels which enjoy increasingly good business. You can even choose the 'size of day' (number of birds in the bag) according to your pocket as the skilled shoot operator can easily tailor the day's success. If you wish you can pay by the day (sometimes with a surcharge for birds shot beyond a certain bag), so much per bird for the entire bag or one sum to include both shooting and holiday.

A small number of Guns take let days extensively, preferring the constant change of scenery and variety of faces to what they see as boredom over many years with the same syndicate on the same patch.

But there is an ugly side to commercialism. While most sporting agents and shoot proprietors have good reputations and consistently provide value for money, there is a tiny minority after the 'quick buck', who fail to deliver the goods for visitors who they believe will never come back. Common complaints are that bags are lower than expected (even allowing for poor marksmanship), the land is greatly overshot, the care of wildlife and landscape are pathetic and atmosphere lacking. Fortunately the shooting 'grapevine' is extensive and usually brings about the rogues' rapid demise. But a reasonable attitude must be adopted towards bags of migratory birds as they are obviously unpredictable. Refunds may be negotiable.

Such let days also enable you to try quarry such as capercaillie and black grouse, which most Guns would not normally encounter, and they are also available for all forms of walked-up shooting. Again, the shooting magazines are a good source of contacts, though nothing is better than a trusted friend's recommendation.

In comparing the value of let days, it is worth remembering that while more distant shoots may be cheaper, the overall cost of a shooting holiday will be considerably more when expensive petrol and extra overnight accommodation are allowed for. There is also the cost of insurance against cancellation through bad weather or other unforeseen circumstances and it is important to note that the rate of cancellation goes up in wetter and colder northern regions, especially later in the season. For example, one company recently quoted a premium of 8.4 per cent for grouse shooting in October, compared with 3.5 per cent for August, and all pheasant and partridge shooting was covered by a level of 3.85 per cent, except for cold January, when it soared to 15 per cent.

If you are really hard up, probably the easiest way to get a taste of driven shooting is to work hard as a regular beater for a shoot. Then, if you are lucky, you might be invited to the special keeper's day at the end of the season.

## *WILDFOWLING*

Purists would argue that true wildfowling takes place only over coastal waters, but here I will consider both salt- and fresh-water sport. The shooting of geese, duck, and waders offers some of the most exciting and cheapest sport in Britain.

Duck shooting from a "blind". The wildfowler must be proficient in the identification of quarry species in gloomy conditions.

If you want to shoot wildfowl inland then, like the roughshooter or gameshooter, you must either seek the permission of landowners, pay for rights in the open market, or buy days through the agents or other advertisers. However, although duck (especially mallard) are reared and released to increase bags, the bulk of wildfowl are migratory and thus very unpredictable.

Most inland flighting of duck and geese is taken by the gameshooters who sport over the same land, but it is often worthwhile asking a farmer if you can shoot the duck which you have noticed coming into his stubbles just after harvest. But goose shooting has had a lot of bad publicity of late as landowners and agents have over-exploited the resource and allowed far too much shooting over the same areas in order to maximize incomes. There has also been poor control, with birds disturbed at their roosts and continually shot at out of range by 'cowboys' and inexperienced Guns.

The owners and their agents often work in conjunction with sporting hotels and it is very important to establish the shoot's reputation. It is imperative that the sporting hotel is sure of its sporting rights, clearly defines its boundaries, does not encourage excessive bags, draws the attention of novices to the BASC Codes of Practice (see page 168 for their address) and provides them with a responsible host or guide. It should also be made clear which species may be shot and the Gun should be proficient in wildfowl identification as the habitat is shared by many protected species. If possible, go to hostelries recommended by experienced friends.

Most wildfowl flighting takes place on the foreshore. In England, Wales, and Northern Ireland this is the part of the seashore which is more often than not covered by the ebb and flow of the four ordinary tides occurring midway between spring and neap tides. This foreshore may be in Crown or private ownership. However, in England and Wales the BASC has an agreement with the Crown Estate Commissioners whereby BASC members will not be prosecuted for carrying guns on Crown foreshore. This should provide a sound defence if a prosecution is brought for armed trespass.

Over the years parts of the foreshore have been sold or leased by the Crown to clubs, local authorities, companies, private individuals, or institutions such as the National Trust. In many cases the new owner or lessee also has the sporting rights and therefore his permission to shoot there must be obtained. It is the responsibility of the shooter to establish ownership. He must also seek authority to cross private land leading to the foreshore, unless there is a public right of way.

Much of the foreshore is controlled by wildfowling clubs and only their members may shoot there. For most people these clubs provide the best introduction to wildfowling. Even beginners with access to private foreshore would benefit from the strict club discipline.

Most wildfowling clubs are limited to a certain number of members and many have a waiting list, though there is always a steady turnover of members in the larger clubs and you shouldn't have to wait more than a season or two for a vacancy. If you don't know an established member who will propose you then write to the club secretary to ask if there is anyone willing to take you under his wing. Some clubs will require a 'seconder' as well, and during the customary probationary period you may shoot only in the company of either the proposer or seconder.

A probationary member must study attentively and at the end of, say, one year may be called before a sub-committee to demonstrate that he has acquired a good knowledge of quarry identification, shooting law, etiquette, safety, and local boundaries. He must be thoroughly responsible in every way as most of the foreshore and coastal waters are shared by other members of the public—yachtsmen, birdwatchers, etc.—as well as a host of protected birds.

Of the 350 or so clubs affiliated to the BASC, about two-thirds are wildfowling associations, whose membership is usually very reasonable—about £20-£60 per annum including the BASC subscription.

Some clubs also operate day-permit schemes for non-members, but these are always restricted in number and should be applied for as soon as possible. They may stipulate that the visitor must be accompanied by a club member.

In Scotland the foreshore is the area between the high and low water of ordinary spring tides and, except in Orkney and Shetland, whether it is owned by the Crown or privately, the Crown retains in trust certain rights by virtue of which members of the public may engage in wildfowling. In certain cases—nature reserves, for example—the public right may be taken away by statute and again the onus is on the wildfowler to establish whether such exclusion zones exist. As elsewhere in the UK, he must also obtain permission to cross private land leading to the foreshore.

## RABBIT AND PIGEON SHOOTING

Rabbits and pigeons will usually form significant parts of the average roughshooter's bag. The gameshooter too will have plenty of opportunity to shoot these quarry, though 'ground' game (rabbits, hares, etc.) is often ignored on driven birdshoots in the interests of safety. But if you have a keen interest in rabbit or pigeon shooting you would do well to seek out one of the small number of specialist clubs.

Such clubs usually have a small number of members who provide local estates with a valuable, year-round crop-protection service. Subscriptions are mostly very low and include BASC membership, but usually there are waiting lists. It is an advantage to know an existing member and to be able to shoot on any day of the week as soon as the farmer calls for help.

### FURTHER TIPS

If all else fails you could join a clay-pigeon shooting club or simply go along to some of the open clay-shoots which are held regularly in most areas. Among the enthusiasts you will find many gameshooters, roughshooters, and wildfowlers, especially out of season, and befriending them will bring you a great deal of good advice and, with any luck, an invitation or two. At the same time you will improve your marksmanship while awaiting the great day of your first 'live' shoot.

Do not be tempted to buy woodpigeon shooting unless you know something about the operator. In most cases purchasers are very disappointed and have often arrived at distant fields, which they have never seen before, and not fired a single shot. This is hardly surprising as successful pigeon shooting depends on sound local knowledge of crops and bird movements. There have been recent cases where unscrupulous men advertised pigeon shooting at £20-30 per day and made off with a pile of money while droves of naïve shooters hung pathetically around fields which wouldn't attract woodpigeons in a thousand years.

Finally, don't expect your search for shooting to be easy, and remember: parting with large amounts of money cannot guarantee quality. When you do have your own shoot you must work hard at improving it and always look out for further acreages as your host may terminate the arrangement at any time.

## LICENSED TO PROCEED

In order to minimize the risk of accident, reckless behaviour, and unnecessary pressure on wildlife, there are some important legal requirements to which all shooters must conform before setting foot in the field. Every time a gun is misused in violent crime there are calls for tighter gun controls and it is important that the sportsman remains alert to any changes in the law.

### SHOTGUN CERTIFICATES

All the quarry described in this book are killed with a shotgun. To own, use, and buy one a shotgun certificate is usually required. This will be issued by the local police constabulary on payment of the appropriate fee to anyone of the required age who is of sound mind and without a criminal record. At the moment the applicant does not have to provide evidence of where the gun will be used. Neither does he have to own a special security cabinet, though it always makes sense to lock guns up and mandatory security is under review.

A shotgun certificate is not required by the following people:
☐ One carrying a shotgun or ammunition belonging to another person holding a certificate while under instruction from that person and for the use of that other person for sporting purposes only. This

The gameshooter should always carry his shotgun certificate in the field to avoid confrontation with the police.

would include a loader.

☐ One who borrows a shotgun from the occupier of private premises (including land) and uses it on those premises in the occupier's presence.

☐ One who uses a shotgun at a time and place approved for shooting at artificial targets (for example, a clay-shooting ground or shooting school) by the local police.

☐ One who has been in Great Britain for not more than thirty days in the preceding twelve months and possesses, purchases, or acquires a shotgun.

In Northern Ireland a firearms certificate includes shotguns as well as rifles and pistols. Application forms are available from the Chief Constable, Royal Ulster Constabulary, Brooklyn, Knock Road, Belfast BT5 6LE. A holder does not need a shotgun certificate while in England, Scotland, and Wales. Persons holding British shotgun certificates do not need a Northern Ireland firearms certificate while visiting Ulster.

Your shotgun certificate should always be carried in the field to avoid confrontation with the police. Unless you can produce it a constable has every right to seize your gun. Changes of address should be notified to the police and the onus is on the holder to apply for renewal in good time (currently three years).

Gamebirds and wildfowl are traditionally shot only with shotguns, but ground game, including hares and rabbits, and some pests such as squirrels and foxes are also shot with rifles, for which you will need a firearms certificate in England, Scotland, and Wales. This too is obtained from the local police and the applicant will need to show 'good reason' for having one. Usually he must prove that he has somewhere to use the gun and allow the police to inspect his security arrangements. These 'Part I' firearms must be locked up.

## YOUNG PEOPLE AND SHOTGUNS

In England, Scotland, and Wales there is no lower age limit for possession of a shotgun certificate, but there are restrictions on the age at which minors (under eighteen) may possess or purchase shotguns and ammunition:

☐ It is an offence to make a gift of a shotgun or ammunition to a person aged under fifteen. A person under fifteen may not have an assembled shotgun with him except: (i) when he is under the direct supervision of someone aged twenty-one or over, in which case he may use the shotgun under that person's instruction providing he has a shotgun certificate; (ii) when the shotgun is in a securely fastened gun cover so that it cannot be fired.

☐ A person aged fifteen or sixteen may be given or lent a shotgun and ammunition but he may not buy them. He may also use a shotgun without supervision as long as he holds a shotgun certificate.

☐ Anyone aged seventeen or over may purchase a shotgun and ammunition providing he holds a shotgun certificate.

☐ A person under the age of eighteen in Northern Ireland who purchases, acquires, or possesses a firearm or ammunition shall be guilty of an offence except in the following cases and providing he is aged sixteen or more: (i) when he has with him a firearm (including a shotgun) or ammunition for sporting purposes when he is in the company of and supervised by a person aged eighteen or over who holds a firearms certificate in respect of that gun or ammunition; (ii) when he purchases, acquires, or has in his possession a shotgun or any other firearm of a calibre not exceeding .22in and appropriate ammunition for the purpose of destroying or controlling animals or birds: (a) on agricultural land occupied by him; (b) on agricultural lands where he works and on which he lives.

## GAME LICENCES

A game licence must be bought from any Crown Post Office before you can shoot any of the following species: pheasant, grey partridge, redlegged partridge, red grouse, black grouse, ptarmigan, common-snipe, woodcock, and hare. However, you do not need one to shoot hares if you are shooting on land where you are the owner (having the right to kill game), occupier, or a person duly authorized in writing under the provisions of either the Hares Act 1848 or the Ground Game Acts. Only one person can be so authorized and must be either: (i) a member of the occupier's household resident on the land, (ii) a person in the occupier's ordinary service on the land, or (iii) a person genuinely employed for reward to kill and take hares and rabbits on the land.

A game licence currently costs £6 annually for the period 1 August to 31 July, £4 for the period 1 August to 31 October, £4 for the period 1 November to 31 July and £2 for any period of fourteen days. Game licences are very unpopular among sportsmen because the income derived is not put back into shooting and appears to be swallowed up by bureaucracy. However, it should be noted that many commercial shoots now check that visitors have game licences.

It is necessary to have a £4 game dealer's licence to sell game, though a person holding a licence to shoot game may sell it to a licensed dealer.

## INSURANCE

It is only commonsense for the shooter to arrange adequate insurance, even though it is not mandatory. In recent years a number of companies have introduced various policies, some of which cover possessions such as guns and dogs as well as personal injury. Yet by far the most popular is that which comes with BASC membership, providing third-party liability with indemnity up to £1 million.

# SHOOTING INSTRUCTION AND FIELDCRAFT

Once you have access to shooting and the necessary licences and certificates, you will want to make the best of every opportunity. To achieve success you will need to acquire skill in gun handling and, for some types of shooting, fieldcraft. Wide reading will be a great asset but, as ever, there is no substitute for experience.

Irrespective of natural ability, it is always worthwhile taking instruction from a qualified coach, who will provide you with the opportunity to practise on artificial, clay targets.

A good coach will teach you to mount your gun properly and develop good timing and composure. You will learn how to stand well and temper any naturally swift reaction with steadiness. But, while the ability to hit targets consistently may make a champion clayshooter, on its own it does not create a good gameshooter. Fieldcraft, knowledge of the quarry's natural history, and self-restraint are important too. The ability to kill easily and efficiently does not mean that every killing opportunity has to be taken.

Although some prefer to deny it, the hunting instinct is latent in everybody, along with a degree of stealth and, hopefully, common-sense. But learning the many subtleties of fieldcraft in each form of shooting will obviously be quicker under the wing of the experienced Gun. Only in driven shooting is there no real necessity for a great knowledge of fieldcraft, for the birds are presented without the need to seek them in their natural haunts. Nonetheless, most devoted driven shooters will occasionally want to walk-up or stalk game in the old-fashioned way and then basic fieldcraft will be important.

A youngster's first shots should be earned through patience and study of natural history and habitat, and there is no better training ground than a good roughshoot. The first thing that a roughshoot's variety teaches is alertness, for eyes and ears are at once attuned to the expectancy of bolting rabbit, crossing pigeon, exploding pheasant, mallard off the pond, teal springing from the dyke, 'invisible' snipe from that apparently empty, reedy field bottom, the jay swooping across the forest ride, and much besides. And what better booty could the apprentice Gun take home than a selection of such species to examine, admire, eat, and read about. The driven game can come later.

The novice gameshooter will learn a great deal through joining the beaters, to see how various quarry react under stress and to watch the expectant Guns from a bird's eye view. In any case, one day he will have to take his turn as 'walking Gun' in step with the beaters and ought to know their procedure under the gamekeeper's guidance.

In driven shooting you do not have to own a gundog as pickers-up will be provided, but walking-up gamebirds is much more productive if specialist breeds of hunting dog are used. Many people must

Out on the grouse moor: learning the ropes will be much quicker under the wing of an experienced Gun.

content themselves with just one dog and settle for an all-rounder such as a springer spaniel or labrador, both of which will flush and retrieve most types of game and wildfowl. There is plenty of expert advice available in breed selection and this is very important if you intend to shoot alone for much of the time.

Fieldcraft is particularly important in wildfowl shooting, in the pursuit of very restless and unpredictable migratory birds. Fortunately most British wildfowling operates through the club system, which ensures expert guidance by experienced members.

The student club wildfowler will be given much assistance, but in the end he must recognize that all wildfowlers are natural loners and he must not expect others to hand to him on a plate all the local knowledge which has taken them years to accumulate in achieving success. Also he must never stop learning and must remain eager to try new tactics.

The necessary group organization of driven shooting means that tactics are discussed well in advance, but very often the shoot owner or captain will shoulder the burden along with his headkeeper. However, showing an interest in operations will always be appreciated, help to ensure good quality sport, and certainly broaden the Gun's outlook and understanding. All the best shoots are continually experimenting with new drives.

The successful sportsman will know the lives of his quarry intimately, not only for his own fascination, but also so that he may increase his bag. He must know where and when to look, what the quarry feeds on in every season, its habits and preferences, and usual behaviour. Then he must learn how to approach it or entice it within range and kill with minimal disturbance to other quarry and wildlife.

The ability to judge range accurately is particularly important in order to minimize the risk of wounding birds at long range and to avoid taking an unsporting shot and blasting a bird at very short range (which also makes it unpresentable to the cook). It's all very well having very testing, extreme-range birds on a good driven pheasant shoot, but they must be tackled only by competent Guns.

Cartridge manufacturers produce tables showing the approximate killing ranges of their various loads and shot sizes in combination with particular gun barrel chokes. However, even the bigger-bore fowling guns with the most powerful loads gain little more than ten yards or so beyond the reach of the standard gameshooter's 12-bore. Thus today's sporting philosophy is generally to content oneself with the 12-bore's maximum effective range of forty-five yards or so and concentrate on acquiring the fieldcraft to get well within that distance. Thus in all forms of live shooting we are looking to make shots beyond a minimum sporting range but well within the range at which luck plays a part and quarry may escape wounded to die slowly.

The Gun should first practise with clay pigeons and later shoot at

live quarry only within his capabilities. Regular practice in range judging should be undertaken. Try estimating the range of various objects about the countryside and then pacing them out to see how accurate you are. In different lights and weather and over varying terrain it won't be easy, but experience will show the way. And you can devise many ways not to forget. For example, the pheasant shooter may relate his shots to the known height of the tallest trees, the pigeon shooter may put range markers among his decoys, and the wildfowler may pace out the distance of features from his hide.

This is the sort of valuable information which, along with many other tips, will be gained through attending courses run by the shooting organizations, including the Game Conservancy's Young Shots' Courses and the BASC's wildfowling and pigeon-shooting weekends.

# SAFETY AND SECURITY

The shotgun is a lethal weapon and its user must be thoroughly versed in its safe handling and storage. Commonsense dictates that we want to minimize injury to ourselves, but also we must ensure the safety of many other outdoor enthusiasts and do our utmost to prevent our guns falling into the hands of criminals.

Much shooting is carried out in remote places, but even when alone the sportsman must never lapse into carelessness, believing that there is no one else nearby. Behind that hedge could lurk a farmer, forester, rambler, birdwatcher, picnicker, or someone else engaged in fieldsports—a beater, ghillie, stalker, or angler, for example. Always err on the side of safety and persevere with safety measures until they are automatic. Even when cold and tired, do not be tempted to let standards slip: remain alert and self-disciplined.

Never assume that your shooting companions are safe and beware of picking up bad habits from associates. If you see someone behaving dangerously then tell him, politely but firmly, where he is going wrong. If there is no immediate danger take him to one side and speak privately so that he is not embarrassed in front of other companions.

The overwhelming majority of shotgun users have an excellent safety record but every time an incident occurs the anti-gun lobby seizes on it. Similarly, whenever shotguns figure in armed crime we can be sure that at least some sections of the police and public will call for tighter controls, even though we know that such measures would have little impact on crime. Thus we must be on our toes to ensure that shotguns remain an acceptable part of everyday British life.

An excellent grounding in safety and security is provided by the voluntary Proficiency Award Scheme run by the British Association for Shooting and Conservation. The Game Conservancy's Young Shots' Courses will help too.

## *GUN HANDLING*

Immediately check if a gun is loaded whenever you pick it up, put it in a vehicle, gun case or slip, or enter a building—even if it is handed to you by a friend. Most people forget to unload at some time.

Never point a gun at anyone or anything other than your quarry, even if unloaded.

After loading your gun, close it by bringing the stock upwards while pointing the barrels safely to the ground. This will prevent accidents should the gun malfunction and discharge on closure.

Always unload your gun when negotiating an obstacle such as a ditch, hedge, or fence. It is not enough to break your gun as injury and death have occurred when sportsmen fell, their loaded guns shut on impact with the ground, and the shock fired the cartridges left in the breech.

When in company, always carry the empty gun over the crook of your arm, with the breech open. You will still see quite a few sportsmen, usually rather elderly, who persist in talking to you with their closed guns pointing at your feet, but they are a dying breed. Reject their arguments about this being better for the gun, for safety must always override everything.

Before passing a gun to someone always open the breech and pass the stock first. If you must pass the gun closed then first open it to show the recipient that it is empty.

When you are shooting, the unbroken gun should be carried in one of the following ways: (i) with the breech resting on the shoulder, the trigger guards uppermost, and the barrels pointing skywards; (ii) over the crook of your arm with barrels pointing to the ground; (iii) held firmly with both hands and the barrels pointing forward and towards the ground or skywards.

Only load your gun when you are about to start shooting.

When walking-up game or waiting for driven birds, only point your gun where you are looking and where it is absolutely safe. When turning in a line of Guns to take a shot behind, always point the muzzle skywards and never swing your gun 'through the line'.

Never release the safety catch until you are mounting the gun and intend to fire it. Do not slip the safety catch off when you see a distant bird approaching. It may change its mind and you may forget that the gun is not on safe. No time is lost by waiting till you are mounting the gun. A sudden jarring can cause a gun to fire even when on 'safe'.

Although few are used today, old hammerguns are potentially more dangerous and it is particularly important not to cock the hammers until about to fire and to keep your fingers well away from them. They can be awkward to operate when wet and cold and can easily get snagged in branches or even the user's jacket.

When expecting to shoot, always keep the forefinger along the trigger guard or in some equally safe and convenient position, but

never inside the guard near the trigger as it is easy to fire prematurely in all the excitement.

When unloading, turn away from your companions and point the barrels towards the ground. Always open a hammergun and remove the cartridges before uncocking, pointing the barrels at the ground.

Never stand your gun where it may slip or be accidentally knocked over and never lay your gun down unbroken.

Never shoot unless you are well-balanced on both feet and otherwise secure and composed.

## CONDUCT IN THE FIELD

Never shoot where you cannot see: vegetation can easily conceal a beater, dog-handler, or walker.

Never shoot towards highways, public footpaths within range, farmhouses, or other buildings.

Always let the farm manager and his staff know when and where you will be shooting.

Make sure you know the positions of shooting companions and that they know exactly where you are! Do not assume that your host or shoot captain has already told them.

Do not hesitate to ask your host to explain anything that is not clear.

When shooting on shared ground, as in roughshooting or wildfowling, always enquire if other shooters are in the vicinity.

Keep in a straight line when walking with Guns and beaters.

Beware of ricochets when shooting at low-flying or ground game or across water. And remember the range or carrying power of your ammunition. Small shot may carry over 270 yards.

Check your barrels frequently for blockages. Soft substances such as mud and snow can cause a burst and you could lose a hand or eye.

Never use a gun—especially a borrowed weapon—unless you clearly understand how it works, especially with regard to safety catches and self-loading mechanisms.

Never shoot while under the influence of medicines or alcohol, which may cause drowsiness or other dangerous conditions.

Never shoot unless fully fit and well.

Never attach a dog's lead to you as it may pull you off balance.

## DRIVEN GAMESHOOTING

Always remember that the safety of your companions comes before your sporting satisfaction.

Never move from your allocated position unless making a fine adjustment within the sight of neighbouring Guns and approved by your host.

Be very careful to determine safe firing angles before shooting commences. The line of Guns may curve considerably, partially hidden by trees, and in grouse shooting Guns may be at varying

The gameshooter must be careful not to swing through the line of Guns and never "poach" his neighbours' birds.

41

heights across the hill. If there are no markers in your butt, shoot only within forty-five degrees to the left and right of a line to your front.

Always unload between drives. Put your empty gun in a sleeve if you have one. This will also make it easier to carry and protect it from knocks and scratches.

Make sure you know from which direction the beaters will approach and what the signals are to begin and stop firing—often a whistle or horn. Also find out where the stops, flankers, and pickers-up are. The latter often stand close behind the line and may move about.

If you are shooting with a pair of guns, you and your loader should practise with unloaded weapons before shooting begins. Each gun should be handed to you and returned with the safety catch on. If, after firing one shot only, the shooter intends to pass the gun back to his loader, he should put the safety catch on again.

Don't shoot at low birds: not only is it unsporting but also the beaters may be in danger towards the end of a drive.

Be particularly vigilant if a woodcock appears as it often creates great excitement and is a notorious cause of accidents, jinking through the coverts at head height.

If you are not sure, ask if ground game and foxes may be shot. Fast-running animals are often ignored in covert, where they may easily lead to accidents, but a Gun in a field may take them where he has a clear view.

Never take chances, no matter what neighbouring Guns may think of your reactions.

## ROUGHSHOOTING

Before you set out make sure you know exactly where you are allowed to go and where the boundaries are on each piece of land.

As your sport will be mainly informal and of a walked-up nature, it is imperative that you are constantly aware of the whereabouts of your companions and their dogs and observe safe shooting angles.

Do not fire your gun near livestock as you may distress the animals.

When lofting pigeon decoys beware of power lines.

On hare drives beware of the large number of inexperienced Guns brought in to make up numbers. Some of them are likely to get over-excited and swing right through the advancing line.

Never shoot from a moving vehicle—when rabbiting at night, for example—as injuries and even deaths have occurred in this way.

## WILDFOWLING

Before you shoot over a section of coast for the first time visit it in daylight with someone who knows it well, to familiarize yourself with boundaries and local dangers such as deep mud and creeks which fill rapidly with the incoming tide.

Always tell someone else where you are going and when you expect to return so that the alarm may be raised if necessary.

Respect the speed of the incoming tide and always leave plenty of time to regain the safety of the seawall. Allow for tidal variations due to weather conditions.

Take food and drink for a long day. If you are marooned you will need all your energy. Wear warm, waterproof clothing, also to conserve your strength.

Beware of nearby shooters who may have already gone out on the marsh under cover of darkness.

Wear a waterproof wristwatch to establish the state of the tide and carry a pocket compass as it is easy to lose your sense of direction in a wilderness of mud and water, especially at night or in fog. Note the bearing for a safe return.

Carry flares or a powerful torch to flash in case of emergency. Repeated firing of shots may also summon help, as will a whistle.

Carry a long pole to sound the depth of mud.

If using a gunning punt or a boat to reach your shooting station, make sure it is regularly overhauled and thoroughly sea-worthy. Always carry an anchor, baler, life-jacket, and emergency flares.

## THE GUN

In Britain any new or secondhand gun sold has to meet the standards laid down by the Proof Laws and be appropriately stamped by one of the two British Proof Houses or those of a foreign country with whom Britain has reciprocal arrangements. A professional gunsmith will be able to verify the proof status of a secondhand gun for sale.

Have your gun overhauled annually by a competent gunsmith to ensure it is in good, safe condition. Never use one that has even a slight malfunction.

Do not use a gun with undue movement between the barrels and the action, for when such a gun is fired, back pressure can develop and escape through the gap, causing serious injury to the eyes.

Never use a gun with badly pitted or dented barrels, or which has an over-sensitive 'hair' trigger liable to go off at the slightest touch.

Never use a gun with a faulty safety catch or a rib which has become raised.

Never use a gun with a cracked or badly damaged stock, which may break with recoil and endanger the shooter or others nearby.

## CARTRIDGES

Never mix up the ammunition of guns of different bore. A 20-bore cartridge is easily loaded into a 12-bore gun by mistake and will not fall right through, but will allow a 12-bore cartridge to be loaded behind it, probably resulting in a burst barrel and serious injury to the shooter on firing.

In the event of a misfire, point the barrels at the ground while investigating the cause.

Never attempt to reload cartridges without expert advice and use only reloads which have been made strictly in accordance with recommended powder and shot measures. Never load a cartridge with anything other than properly manufactured lead shot.

Use only those cartridges which conform to the proof limitations as marked on your gun and which are of suitable length.

Never store cartridges under extreme conditions of temperature or humidity as dangerously high pressures can result. Do not dry wet cartridges near a heat source.

Do not store unreasonably large amounts of cartridges in one place but do store them under lock and key.

Always take your empty cartridge cases home or dispose of them safely as, apart from being unsightly, they may be swallowed by animals, possibly causing internal injuries or blockages.

### SECURITY IN THE HOME
Never have a loaded gun indoors.

Whenever possible store your guns in a locked cupboard or cabinet —ideally a purpose-built steel cabinet bolted to the wall in an inconspicuous place (this could well become a statutory requirement as a result of the Firearms (Amendment) Bill in the committee stage at the time of going to press).

Never leave a gun within reach of children—even for a short time—and always store your ammunition separately, also locked away.

If your gun is not locked up, always conceal it and/or dismantle it so that it cannot be fired.

Do not advertise the whereabouts of your guns as their value alone may attract criminals.

Guns should not be left in unoccupied houses for long periods. Your bank or local gunshop should be able to help.

Wall-display guns should be adapted so that they cannot be fired. Note your guns' serial numbers and photograph distinguishing features to help in their recovery should they be stolen.

### SECURITY WHILE TRAVELLING
Never travel with a loaded gun in your vehicle, even between drives on a shoot. Always transport your gun in a case or cover. Should anyone enter your vehicle with an unbroken, uncovered gun then satisfy yourself that it is not loaded.

Avoid leaving a gun in an unattended car. If you must do so for a short time—for example, to break a long motorway journey—then conceal the gun from view, close the windows and lock all the doors.

On no account shoot from a moving vehicle.

It is illegal to have a loaded shotgun in a public place.

# GOOD SPORTSMANSHIP AND ETIQUETTE

Today we no longer play the numbers game. The good sportsman has no interest in trying to emulate the Victorian and Edwardian Big Shots who made excessive bags. Quality and moderation are now paramount and it is our responsibility to safeguard our quarry and its habitat for future generations.

What constitutes a 'reasonable' bag varies with the quarry, method of shooting, custom, local conditions and rules, and, in the case of wild or migratory birds, the success of the breeding season. While the lucky Gun may have the occasional opportunity to shoot 100 'pest' woodpigeons over farmland decoys or thirty to fifty pheasants on a big day, usually he will be properly content with, say, half-a-dozen duck or snipe or just two or three highly prized wild geese. There are no national set rules, though many groups impose their own local restrictions on members. But anyone without respect for our quarry will soon be castigated by fellow Guns and incur the wrath of a concerned public.

It goes without saying that national laws and local rules and customs must be strictly observed, but beyond that the sportsman must demonstrate exemplary behaviour and have the greatest regard for the enjoyment and safety of his fellow Guns in what is a highly organized social activity. There is little satisfaction in being a great Shot if one is regarded as greedy, discourteous, and ignorant of custom.

## DRIVEN GAMESHOOTING

The beginner is often daunted by the apparently impenetrable maze of customs and etiquette surrounding driven gameshooting, which is largely, of necessity, a group sport.

Invitations should always be sent as early as possible as anyone receiving late notice will suspect he is second or third choice, though some substitutes are inevitable.

Dress should be both smart and practical; colours should be sober and blend with the surroundings; and on all but the most informal shoots a shirt and tie (or cravat) are worn.

Try to cater for all weathers so that you are not embarrassed by having to borrow special clothing and footwear, and above all ensure that you are comfortable in unfamiliar surroundings. And, although you may prefer the wind rushing through your hair, you will be the odd one out if you turn up without a hat—a flat cap will do.

Always take plenty of cartridges. If you run out you will be frustrated and your host possibly offended because you underrated his shoot. But do not take so many as to embarrass your host with your over-expectation. An average-sized bag containing 75-100 cartridges should cover most days, but a further, discreet supply in your car (which should be accessible at lunchtime) is advisable. Although less popular among older Guns, a cartridge belt is also useful. And no matter what your companions do, you will set a good example in picking up all your spent cartridges, unless you are lucky enough to have someone do this for you.

Lunch will often be provided, but if your host does not indicate what the form is when inviting you, then do ask. If you must provide your own, then treat yourself well, with a little extra to offer round.

Never take your dog unless it is thoroughly trained, there is a positive role for it, and you have asked permission.

Only shoot with two guns if your host has invited you to and you know that a loader will be available.

Never take along your spouse or a friend, even to watch, without prior permission, as sufficient food and transport must be available.

Be certain that you arrive on time. Park your car where it will not block anyone who may want to leave early (for example at lunchtime) and immediately introduce yourself—always first to your host. A good host will note your arrival and make you welcome, introducing you to all the other Guns.

A good host will address the assembled company. Take note if ground game and foxes are to be shot. Sometimes there will be other restrictions, such as no hen pheasants. On no account digress.

Before shooting begins be certain of your neighbours' positions and on no account poach their birds—those which are clearly closer to them. If many birds flight through 'no man's land', do not take more than your fair share. If safe, it is permissible to take such birds if your neighbour has already missed, but beware of doing it too often as he might then hold back an invitation for you to shoot with him!

If there are 'back Guns' in a second row, let them have their fair share of sport as they are not only there to 'mop up' where you have missed. Take care to leave birds still rising which may be only marginally sporting for you, as these will inevitably go on to present more worthy marks for those behind. If there is doubt about who shot a bird, resist the temptation to claim it and congratulate your neighbour on his shot.

Be as quiet as possible when you move between pegs and never boast of your exploits. Help other Guns to cross obstacles such as ditches and fences. Hold their guns when necessary and do not rush to take the best seats on shoot vehicles.

Never shoot before the signal to start a drive and never shoot after that which ends it. Unload immediately and move smartly to your next allotted position, with your gun broken or covered.

Resist the temptation to shoot immature birds or those which are unsportingly low, even if your neighbours are less fussy.

Try to remember how many birds you have down and where they fall. This will make the task of pickers-up much easier and speed the day along. Put dogs onto 'runners' (wounded birds) first.

Never leave wounded birds flapping in pain near your peg. In the event of a picker-up or other assistant not being on hand to despatch such a bird immediately you should stop shooting and (provided it is safe) do the job yourself. A sharp knock on the head with a 'priest' (which performs the 'last rites') or suitably heavy stick is most effective for birds. Rabbits and hares can be killed by holding them by the head between the first and second fingers, with the first finger under the creature's chin, and quickly jerking the animal downwards, thus dislocating the neck.

It is customary to tip the headkeeper at the end of the day. Hopefully, he will share contributions among all the keepers. Unfortunately, today tips are still generally related to numbers in the bag and many Guns stick rigidly to a system of, say, £10 for the first 100 birds plus £5 for each 100 thereafter. There is much that can affect the bag and which is beyond the keeper's control—weather, marksmanship, etc. Yet he has still put in the same great effort before the day. If in doubt, consult your host. In the end it boils down to what you can afford, but do remember that many keepers are not well paid. Whatever you give, hand it over discreetly (you will often be handed the customary brace at that point), shake the keeper by the hand, and thank him warmly for his efforts.

If you have a loader, you will have to tip him too.

At the end of it all try to make a point of saying goodbye to *all* the Guns. Thank the beaters if they are still around and, lastly, thank your host most sincerely and do not overstay at any shoot supper.

The very next day write to your host to say how much you enjoyed yourself and to thank him for his hospitality.

Hosts should liaise with neighbouring estates over shoot dates, to avoid unnecessary quarry disturbance or boundary conflicts.

## *ROUGHSHOOTING*

Always inform the landowner and/or farm manager when you intend to shoot and ask if it is convenient.

Never stray onto neighbouring land without prior permission. Always leave your gun behind unless authorized to take it.

If you share land with other shooters, always consult them about convenient dates, in the interests of safety, courtesy, and making the most of your resources. If there is a formal gameshoot on the same land take care to liaise with the gamekeeper.

Shoot only those species which the landowner has mentioned.

Whenever possible use a gundog to retrieve game, which may be wounded. Without pickers-up it is up to you to despatch all wounded quarry as quickly as possible.

Never shoot at quarry over the boundary.

Do not 'feed-in' neighbours' birds without any attempt at your own rearing-and-release programme.

Remember to save part of the bag for the landowner or farm manager who gave you permission to shoot.

Do not cut vegetation or alter the habitat without permission. Always leave the land as tidy as you found it, dismantling hides unless you have permission to leave them standing for another day.

Remember to thank the landowner and/or farm manager regularly and try to offer them something from the bag.

## WILDFOWLING

Know your boundaries well. On club, public, or other shared marshes always try to find out where and when other Guns will be shooting. If someone beats you to your favourite spot then stifle your disappointment and find another position at a discreet distance. Do not intercept the flightlines anticipated by other Guns.

If you arrive too late for the beginning of a flight, do not go on to the marsh to spoil the sport of any other Guns already there.

Always be courteous to other marsh users, who may include ramblers, birdwatchers, and yachtsmen who have every right to be there. Avoid shooting birds while members of the public look on.

Avoid shooting birds which, although legal quarry, may be locally rare. This is often the cause of bad publicity.

Always shoot with a gundog. Whether wounded or dead, birds left unretrieved in public places are bound to create antagonism.

Never overshoot a marsh. Nearby residents will be upset by too much gunfire and the birds (which may be disturbed simply by your presence) will be unduly stressed, especially near roosts.

Shoot only at birds which are comfortably within range as range judging is particularly difficult over featureless areas or in bad light conditions. Think of neighbouring Guns in allowing groups of birds to come well in before firing. In this way everyone may get a shot.

Retrieve each bird as it is shot, unless dead and very close on dry ground.

Never leave unsightly pit holes, seats or other equipment on the marsh.

Never shoot birds weakened or otherwise disadvantaged by severe weather. Such opportunities are most likely to arise in the run-up to a statutory national suspension brought on through continuous severe frost.

Do not use to unfair advantage adjacent artificial lighting from streets and buildings.

Never shoot wildfowl with a rifle.

Avoid disturbance of non-quarry species and of all species at their roosts. Roost flighting should be infrequent and take place at dawn, if at all.

Wear inconspicuous clothing to match your surroundings. Bright colours will not only spoil your chances, but those of neighbouring Guns too.

Never shoot at any bird whose identity is in doubt. Murky conditions at dawn and dusk require special care.

Never shoot any wildfowl which will not be eaten or which may not be retrieved.

## CHOOSING A GUN

Ideally a gun should be chosen to suit a particular form of shooting. However, many sportsmen or beginners can afford only one gun, so if they wish to participate in as many forms of shooting as possible then obviously this single gun must be versatile. The wealthier Shot can consider guns for all occasions, but unnecessary switching of guns from one day to the next is not recommended as it often spoils the user's performance.

Fortunately, the basic, modern 12-bore is a gun for most occasions and is widely available, with choices of features best suited to your needs and fancies. A double-barrelled 12-bore will enable its owner to participate in all forms of gameshooting and roughshooting as well as most wildfowling. It can also be used for clay-pigeon shooting, but if highly competitive target shooting is the main interest then I would recommend specialist 12-bore models.

Persons of slight build or youngsters may prefer to use the smaller 16- or 20-bores, which have less recoil yet sufficient punch to get by on most occasions. However, they are not guns for the serious wildfowler.

The quarry shooter's 12-bore will have the standard two barrels side-by-side or the more modern over-and-under. Effectively there is little difference, though the latter is generally heavier. Weight can be a handicap when carrying a gun for long periods, as in roughshooting, but it is also useful in absorbing recoil—hence the over-and-under's popularity among clay-shooters, who fire many shots in a short time. Some people prefer the side-by-side for steady swinging and its flat, wide sighting plane, while others insist that the over-and-under is easier to get onto birds with and more comfortable to hold. The important thing is to try both and choose that with which you feel most confident. But your choice will be restricted by the range of models available in your price range.

A single-barrel gun is temptingly cheap for youngsters and beginners, but in the end it will prove to be a false economy for anyone who takes shooting seriously. For a start, it is useless in driven gameshooting, when the firing of two shots without reloading is frequently necessary.

Most modern 12-bores are hammerless, with automatic safety catches, which return to 'safe' after a gun is opened to reload. Manual safeties are much more dangerous and are only really useful in some forms of clay-shooting.

Some people find a single trigger faster on a double-barrelled gun, but the trigger finger must momentarily clear the trigger between shots to enable the mechanism to operate properly. Others insist that the conventional double triggers, with the front usually firing the right-hand ('closer range') barrel first, are equally fast.

Most single-trigger guns have a selective mechanism which enables you to choose the order in which the barrels are fired. This is necessary because most guns have different 'choke' in each barrel. Choke is the degree to which the muzzle end of the barrel is constricted. The tighter the choke the greater the distance over which the shot pattern holds together. Thus tightly choked barrels are more suitable for longer-range shots, to maximize the chances of a sufficient number of pellets striking a quarry in vital parts. However, tight choke does not increase the range of a shotgun. It merely increases the chances of a clean kill at long range. A gun's ability to throw a good shot pattern is more important. The five degrees of choke are: full (the tightest), ¾, ½, ¼, and ⅛ (often called 'improved cylinder'). No restriction at the muzzle is known as 'true cylinder'.

A popular combination of chokes among Guns who dabble in most forms of quarry shooting is ¼ in the right barrel for closer shots and ¾ in the left for more distant shots. Guns interested only in driven gameshooting often opt for the more open chokes—improved cylinder and true cylinder—when they expect most shots at moderate range and have confidence in their shot pattern. But such a gun would be pretty useless for the serious wildfowler and roughshooter who need a denser shot pattern at longer range much more frequently if they are to be consistent in placing sufficient pellets on the target.

Pattern is the distribution of pellets in a given circle at a given range, the most dense being produced by full choke and the most open by true cylinder. A combination of full and ½ choke is popular among wildfowlers, whose quarry is mostly very wary and relatively strong and well-feathered.

Many off-the-shelf new guns are available in a variety of chokes, while others can easily be bored out. However, while choke can be removed, it cannot be replaced. The only exception is recess choke, which is usually found only in top-class shotguns. Some guns are available with variable choke devices, but fiddling around with these can lead to erratic performance by the shooter.

Another variable is the gun's length of chamber—that part of the barrel into which the cartridge is inserted. Most 12-bores are chambered for 2½ in or 2¾ in cartridges. It is dangerous to fire a 2¾ in cartridge in a gun chambered for 2½ in cartridges. The longer cartridge is most useful in wildfowling, when heavier loads are required. Light-recoil 2 in cartridges and magnum 3 in cartridges are also available for suitably chambered guns. For safety's sake, it is essential that shotgun and cartridge are compatible. Usually, there will be sufficient information stamped on the gun, cartridge, and cartridge box, but if in doubt consult your local gunshop.

There is also a choice of barrel length with most guns. Today the most popular is 28 in and few people continue with the very long barrels beloved of our forefathers, who wrongly believed barrel length increased range. However, some people prefer extra length for its steadying effect, reducing 'muzzle flip', and opt for the commonly available 30 in. The minimum legal barrel length is 24 in, though standard game guns are rarely made with barrels under 25 in. The shorter barrels are most useful for those who shoot driven game, who value a gun's lightness and swift handling in taking a high percentage of closer shots.

An ejector to throw out the fired cartridges when the gun is opened will save precious time in driven gameshooting when birds come over in quick succession. This device adds to the price of the gun. It is less important to the roughshooter and can be a hindrance for the wildfowler who generally takes only occasional shots and does not want to grope around in the mud or darkness for spent cases. In any event, the non-ejector lifts empty cases slightly, making manual extraction easier. Pump-action and semi-automatic guns automatically eject spent cases and move the next cartridge into the chamber.

Stocks and fore-ends also come in a variety of styles, but the most popular stock remains the 'straight-hand', traditional English. A pistol or semi-pistol grip stock is more suited to a single-trigger gun. American-style 'beaver-tail' fore-ends are wide and, for some at least, comfortable in the hand, but they appear inelegant on a classic English game gun.

Whatever styling you choose, it is essential that your gun fits you properly. If you have a gun made specially for you, the gunsmith will automatically take your measurements and ensure a good fit, but if you buy off-the-shelf or secondhand you may need to get the stock length altered by a gunsmith. He will also bend or 'cast' the stock to suit any special requirements. At the same time, determine which is your master eye: if it is your right, you should shoot from your right shoulder, or vice versa.

Modern gun manufacture continues a very fine and ancient tradition, both home and abroad. Investment-wise, it pays to spend as much as possible on a new gun, especially a 'best' English, which holds its price well, but at the very cheapest end of the market even the most basic import costing under £200 will usually be a thoroughly reliable and tough tool. Irrespective of price, all must conform to safety regulations and be legally stamped as having passed Proof (see page 43).

Mass-production guns are cheap because machine processes are widely employed, whereas bespoke guns can cost tens of thousands of pounds because they are largely hand-crafted and engraved. The use of the finest French walnut for stock and fore-end and precious metals in the action further adds to the price, but the adornment of a gun will not make it shoot straighter.

Whatever gun you choose, it is essential that it is cleaned thoroughly after every shoot, and at the end of every season it is a good idea to have it overhauled by a gunsmith. This will ensure that it is maintained in safe condition, reduce the risk of malfunction, and protect its value. Cleaning kits are widely available from gunshops.

## CARTRIDGES

First ensure that the cartridge is of a suitable length for your gun's chamber. It is unquestionably dangerous to use cartridges which are too long as excessive pressure may result in a burst barrel, but a cartridge which is too short is also bad in that gases may escape around the 'drive' wad and cause erratic performance. Cartridges more than ¼ in short can cause 'balling' of the shot—a particularly dangerous phenomenon.

From the many makes of cartridge available choose those recommended by friends or by a gunsmith for their consistency. Most makes are reliable nowadays, only a few foreign ones having dubious reputations.

Today most cartridge cases are made of plastic or other waterproof material so that they do not swell and prevent insertion into the chamber when damp. However, 'paper' (cardboard) cases are still available and are preferred by those who care for the environment and insist on bio-degradable materials. In any event, cartridge cases should always be disposed of responsibly. Increasingly, care of the environment is also expressed through purchase of cartridges with felt or other bio-degradable wads and shotcups, rather than plastic, which will not rot.

The standard 12-bore game cartridge 2½ in long throws a load of 1¹/₁₆ oz of lead shot. But loads range from a hefty 2 oz in the wildfowler's 8-bore down to a .410's ⁵/₁₆ oz. Different loads are often available for the same length and make of cartridge, the lighter ones being preferred for their reduced recoil, providing performance is adequate. Wildfowlers often use a load of 1¼ oz in a 2¾ in cartridge or even 1⅝ oz in a 3 in cartridge. Many special loads are available for the clay-shooter, though most can be used on game, providing the shot size is appropriate. Some have plated shot, which is harder, and others are high-velocity. But the gun's weight should match the cartridge load. Reduced recoil means quicker recovery to take a second shot.

Shot comes in a variety of sizes appropriate for various quarry: the larger the quarry the larger the shot. In Britain the recommendations are: geese BB, 1, or 3; capercaillie 3, 4, 5; hare 4 or 5; most duck 4, 5, 6; crow 4, 5, 6; rabbit 5 or 6; pheasant 5, 6, 7; grouse, partridge, pigeon, squirrel, teal, and woodcock 6 or 7; snipe 7 or 8. You do not have to stick rigidly to these, but keeping as close as possible will increase your chances of success. For example, trying to hit the tiny snipe is far easier with the 1¹/₁₆ oz load's average 478 size-8 pellets than the same load's average 149 of size 3. Unnecessarily large shot should be avoided as it can lead to smashing the quarry, making it unfit for the table. On the other hand, the shot should be large enough to retain sufficient striking energy and penetration at sensible ranges.

In Britain all shot used on live quarry is still made from lead, but there is increasing opposition to this as the toxicity of lead has resulted in wildlife deaths, particularly among wildfowl which mistakenly ingest the shot when feeding on plant seeds. In the USA steel shot is sometimes used, but advocates of lead point to the latter's superior carrying capacity and stress that the British gun industry would have to re-equip to cope with steel. Unfortunately, steel shot would wear away traditional gun barrels more quickly.

# DRESSED FOR THE FIELD

As most shooting takes place in winter it is essential that you have warm, waterproof clothing available. But it is equally important that you are comfortable, in particular with good footwear to suit much walking over rough ground and a topcoat that allows free arm movement. At the same time you should pay heed to custom and at least try to look smart so that you do not feel out of place, though there is no need to insist on the latest fashion. Choosing an outfit to blend with the surroundings is much more important.

Thankfully, today's sportsmen are not hidebound by fashion as our forefathers were, but it is important to take note of the customs on individual shoots, where Guns may span several generations and have widely varying attitudes. Fitting in really is important. Tatty but loved garments may be acceptable among friends on a small roughshoot, but as a guest you should always look smart.

On the other hand you do not want to look too groomed: the weather-beaten, slept-in look implies that you have been around the coverts more than once and really know your business. Thus a crinkled Barbour with the odd small rip or bloodstain is all right in most circles but an open shirt and yellow anorak certainly are not. On most driven shoots the custom is to wear a suitable traditional shirt and tie, or perhaps a cravat or neckerchief.

The choice of waterproof jackets is now very wide, though from a distance the preponderance of muted-green waxed cotton and wellies gives the impression of a uniform—something no one likes. The name Barbour has become synonymous with waxed cotton—just like Hoover with vacuum cleaner—but suddenly there are many other makes, both cheaper and dearer. They are mostly reliable and hardwearing, though the seams on some I have tried have let in more than a drop of rain.

However, waxed cotton jackets are not perfect. Even with ventilation holes they fail to 'breathe' properly and can be very uncomfortable when the wearer perspires freely during strenuous exercise. They also become very stiff when cold and are not particularly warm. Thus we now have a small but rapidly increasing range of jackets made of materials such as Goretex, which are said to keep all rain out but at the same time allow perspiration to escape. Unfortunately, such jackets are usually more expensive.

Other jackets—mostly of nylon or similar man-made materials—rustle excessively. Not only is this irritating but it can also scare your quarry away.

You will always want plenty of pockets. The two main patch pockets should be spacious, with securely fastening flaps. Ideally there should be a large, washable inside game pocket, a small, waterproof, zip-up pocket in the lining, where money and documents such as shotgun certificate and game licence may be stored securely, and two side-opening breast pockets to slip the hands into when cold.

To be really windproof, the main fastening should be by zip overlapped by studs and the sleeves should have adjustable storm cuffs. A detachable lining and a collar of corduroy or other warm material will further increase comfort. Some jackets also have a waterproof, internal backflap which can be let down when the wearer wants to sit on a wet surface.

Some full-length waxed cotton and other coats are also available, and these are fine for more leisurely driven shooting where there is little climbing of fences or other negotiation of obstacles.

Serious wildfowlers care little for fashion. They often have an old three-quarter length coat which provides extra warmth and camouflage, especially when painted to suit the particular marsh or shoreline. Some fowlers and pigeon shooters also keep an old, long, white cotton coat for those rare days of deep snow, when traditional greens and browns would stand out like sore thumbs. Fortunately, driven gameshooters need not bother with the baker's cast-offs as their quarry is less wary.

The wildfowler who spends hours lying in a pit may welcome an old-fashioned rubber or oilskin coat, but such garments are hopeless to walk in because perspiration condenses on the inside and soon wets the wearer, making him thoroughly uncomfortable. Whatever his coat, the wise wildfowler will as often as possible carry it during the strenuous walk out over the mud to his chosen flighting station.

Waterproof leggings or over-trousers are essential for most shooting, especially where the Gun has to walk through wet, standing crops. They also protect against gorse and brambles. There are many types available. Very popular are stud-fastening, waxed cotton leggings, which are relatively heavy, but my own preference is for lighter over-trousers made from one of the tough modern materials and with an elasticated waist. As long as the bottoms are wide enough to go over your boots, these are much quicker and easier to pop on and off during changing conditions. However, the short leggings are better for minimizing perspiration.

Wellington boots in suitable shades of green or brown are now made by many companies, the best-known of which are Hunters. They should be at least calf-length and ideally with a narrow leg to avoid chafing. The foot should be snug, allowing for thick woollen socks, as any looseness will soon cause blisters. Avoid rubbers which are very soft as they rip easily on barbed wire and can burst at a simple knock on the ankle. Adjustable straps are not necessary. Obviously, waterproof over-trousers should be worn outside of boots.

Long boots are also available in all-leather or part-rubber/part-leather, with various fancy linings. Some are very good indeed and mostly worth the very high prices, but others are mere gestures to

British shooters carry on the great tradition of practical smartness, but today it is hard to tell Gun from beater, picker-up or keeper.

fashion and need close scrutiny. For some shooting, such as walking-up ptarmigan or grouse on treacherous, rocky slopes, good quality, waterproof, ankle-length leather boots are best. Their stoutness supports the ankle well, their superior grip helps to avoid accidents, and they do not cause the intense sweating which such exercise would produce in rubber boots. However, it is essential that leather boots are gently and thoroughly broken in. Never undertake a long hike in new boots. Also take care to choose a lightweight pair, as all the best-quality ones will be. You will also then have footwear which is far warmer than any rubber boot.

Wildfowlers will also need a pair of thigh-length waders for the occasions when they have to cross creeks, trudge through deep mud, or kneel down in ambush. Waders should have top straps which are fastened to your belt to prevent them falling down, which the soft, green rubber ones are likely to do. Even well-fitting waders may be pulled off by deep, sucking mud. Many fowlers prefer black waders or even paint their own for better camouflage.

It is customary to wear a hat for all types of shooting. This is not only fashionable but also practical as without one sooner or later you will get drenched—either by falling rain or the wet which almost permanently fills winter woodland. For driven shooting a smart, tweed cap is popular, but spectacle wearers will benefit from a wide-brimmed hat, which I prefer anyway as it helps to stop rain driving down your collar and covers the face better when you are after a very shy quarry such as duck or pigeon.

Many caps and hats are also available in waxed cotton and other waterproof materials, and since the recent explosion of interest in outdoor clothing, many of these are very smart as well as practical. Jacket hoods and balaclavas are all very well in the most severe cold, but generally they are a hindrance in restricting movement, vision, and hearing.

Beneath the outer shell, the trend is towards a smaller number of layers of clothing which retain insulating layers of warm air rather than masses of tight-fitting, movement-restricting woollies which lose heat rapidly through conduction.

For the coldest days a set of thermal underwear is advisable, the long legs being particularly welcome. Next comes a thick woollen or moleskin shirt—never nylon or similar man-made material which could make you sweat and chill as the perspiration condenses. Above this a well-fitting, heavy-duty woollen sweater, and finally a quilted waistcoat, of which the variety is enormous. But beneath a topcoat you will want to avoid the very thick waistcoats which restrict movement. Your choice should not gape around the arms, but be reasonably well contoured to the body and capable of being buttoned up high. Waxed cotton types are pointless as waistcoats are not outer garments for wet weather.

Trousers come in many materials, but the heaviest are not necessarily the warmest. Among the most popular are tweeds and moleskins, but they become very heavy when waterlogged and on a long day every ounce saved is an appreciable help. For the same reason the good old Harris Tweed jackets are now rarely seen as outer garments, except on balmy grouse-moor days.

The grouse moor calls for rather different clothing at the start of the season, in August, when even northern days can be surprisingly hot. The custom is still to look smart, though sadly in recent times many visiting Guns feel that they can do as they please.

A tweed shooting suit is ideal for August grouse, a fitting accompaniment for colourful heather and blue skies. And on those hot days thin stockings are more comfortable. Studded brogues are more elegant and lighter than wellingtons, but they will not keep your feet dry when you accidentally walk into one of the bogs and pot holes which abound on most moors. However, they really do complement a tailor-made tweed suit with knickerbockers—sometimes called breeks or plus-twos. In fact, some people prefer breeks for all gameshooting, though they are never so wide as the old-fashioned plus-fours which are impractical for much walking and snag the undergrowth.

Both men and ladies also look well in corduroy, moleskin, or loden cloth breeks. The latter is surprisingly water-resistant and also makes excellent jackets and capes, which are greatly favoured on the Continent.

As more and more Continental Guns discover the glories of British gameshooting the variety of field fashion grows—and very welcome it is, especially among the ladies, who take part in the sport less frequently. As spectators, their fashion is understandably at least as important as practicality and they readily encourage the designers' newfound interest in outdoor clothing.

We have come a long way since the beaters wore smocks with letters on and a man's station was apparent from the way he dressed. Today on many shoots it is hard to tell Gun from beater, picker-up, or keeper, for all types engage in all these activities, taking the greatest pleasure simply in being outdoors. The overwhelming majority carry on the great British tradition of practical smartness—a perfect complement to good sportsmanship.

Newcomers to shooting, without friends for advice, can consult their local sports outfitters as to what to wear on that first guest-Gun day. Even in London, there is a wealth of experience and a wide choice of clothing available at the showrooms of the famous gunmakers such as Purdey and Holland and Holland. In addition, the shooting journals regularly carry advertisements for outdoor clothing as well as special features reviewing new products. As always, the more expensive items generally provide better value in the long run.

# GUNDOGS AND SHOOTING ACCESSORIES

Many people would argue that, after the gun and cartridge, the gundog is the most important piece of shooting 'equipment', though it is not necessary for every Gun to own one. The main exception is in driven gameshooting, where the line of beaters replaces questing dogs and standing Guns are relieved of the task of gathering shot birds by (in the main) paid pickers-up and their retrievers.

Nonetheless, even fanatical driven gameshooters usually own a gundog as sooner or later most of them discover the delights of roughshooting or wildfowling alone, for which activities a dog is essential. The Gun must be certain that most of his kills will be retrieved and, more importantly, that wounded birds will be captured and killed as quickly as possible. A gundog will soon scent game that we might spend hours searching for by day and never find at all after dark. It will think nothing of retrieving across mud and from water where we prefer not to venture.

Whatever breed of gundog is chosen, it should have a sound working background and preferably be bred from genuine working and field-trial strains. Ideally it should be a specialist for the type of shooting chosen. However, most people are restricted to one dog and must choose one which can at least retrieve reasonably well and, preferably, hunt as well.

Smaller breeds such as spaniels may be better at working dense cover but larger ones such as the labrador can stand cold better and retrieve heavier game more easily.

For general roughshooting, walking-up, and a spot of pigeon and duck shooting, English springer and cocker spaniels are ideal. These exuberant dogs have great stamina and courage and no hestitation in tackling the thickest, thorniest cover to put out game. The springer is enormously popular, very easily obtained and, above all, trainable.

Driven gameshooters and wildfowlers need a retrieving dog which spends most of its time sitting quietly to heel, one which is not generally required to quest for game. For them the most popular choice is the labrador, a very steady and efficient dog, a strong swimmer and again easily trained. Golden retrievers are a good second choice, and much farther behind, in third place, comes the flatcoat, sometimes regarded as less intelligent and more independent, and thus less easy to train.

'HPR's (breeds which hunt, point, flush, and retrieve) are popular as all-rounders and are widely bred in Britain, following adoption from their Continental stronghold. However, they are less easy to train and often only respond well to a strong master. Critics say such a dog is 'Jack of all trades but master of none'. The best-known is the German shorthaired pointer, but Hungarian vizslas, Munsterlanders, Weimaraners, and Brittany spaniels are also quite easily obtained.

Laying out the pheasants: traditionally the numbers of cocks and hens are recorded in the shoot's gamebook.

For more specialist work such as walking-up grouse moors, ranging over wide tracts of land, and indicating game by pointing, the English pointer and English, Irish, and Gordon setters are unrivalled, but dogs of good working stock are hard to come by. Also, retrievers are needed to back them up.

If you want to train your own dog, then the best course of action is to buy one at eight to twelve weeks old. This will be far cheaper than buying a partly-trained or fully-trained adult dog, which can be a bit of a gamble, especially if not obtained through a friend's recommendation. But before any purchase you must organize adequate kennelling, feeding, and exercise and make sure you can afford it. Working gundogs must be kept very fit indeed. Advice on all aspects of gundogs and their training can be found in specialist books.

A gundog should never be attached to you by a lead when you are shooting and should never be worked in company unless steady and well trained. A badly trained dog can spoil the day for everyone. But they are well worth persevering with as they are almost always excellent and loyal companions. A questing dog will always find more game than you could ever hope to on your own and a retriever will always significantly increase the number of birds in the bag—often by 10 per cent on the grouse moor.

Finally, the shooter should remember that his dog is not a machine and that it will perform better if its comfort is attended to before his own. Always have water available at strategic points on a shoot day, never overtire your dog, never leave it in a car with the windows closed, never send it to retrieve across ice, make sure it is well fed, and always clean it off and dry it thoroughly as soon as possible after shooting has ended. Before you tuck into your shoot lunch in the warm and dry, make sure your dog has a place out of the cold and rain. The wildfowler should try to provide his dog with something to sit on when out on the mudflats.

## ACCESSORIES

The most important accessory for all gun users is a cleaning kit, which must be used after *every* outing to remove the cartridge fouling from inside the barrels and every trace of water. An uncleaned gun will soon rust externally and eventually pits will appear inside the barrels and the internal mechanism will corrode and malfunction.

The basic kit comprises a push rod with screw-on attachments: a jag to push old rags through to remove most of the fouling, a phosphor-bronze brush to remove more difficult leading, and a lambswool brush to apply oil to the internal bores. After thorough drying and cleaning the inside of the barrels, all that is necessary is to lightly oil the outside of the barrels and action with a soft cloth and to rub walnut oil into the stock. Make sure you clean all the crevices around the triggers and trigger guard, the fore-end, top-lever, rib

(especially when ventilated) and exposed parts of the action when the gun is dismantled. A small brush of the type used in dentistry will help and today most people prefer an aerosol of WD40 for the metal parts as it has exceptional penetration, fights corrosion, and does not thicken up to become sticky and clog moving parts.

Regular cleaning will protect the gun's value and minimize the chances of mechanical breakdown. An annual close-season overhaul by a good gunsmith will further increase a gun's life and avoid malfunction on a shoot, thereby improving safety.

The next requirement is for a gun cover or 'sleeve', which will both protect your gun when not in use and enable you to carry it easily by means of a shoulder strap. The cheapest are of man-made materials, while dearer and longer-lasting versions come in canvas and leather or all-leather. A wool or other lining will further protect your gun. Always dry off your gun before putting it into a sleeve.

More expensive guns are supplied with a hard case traditionally made of lined wood and leather, but nowadays sometimes of metal, with compartments which house the disassembled gun and a few accessories. These can also be bought separately to suit most guns. Their main function is to protect the gun in storage and transport. Lockable cases also improve security.

Most people have to carry their own supply of cartridges and for this a purpose-made bag is best on a driven shoot. Most are made of leather or canvas and have 75 or 100-cartridge capacity. Cartridge belts are also useful but usually contain only twenty-five cartridges and are not suitable for use with paper cartridge cases, which may swell in wet weather.

Anyone who ever shoots alone will need a gamebag in which to carry kills. This should have a wide, comfortable, adjustable shoulder strap and a side net in which game may cool.

The pigeon shooter needs a seat for long waits in a hide. In a bale hide a spare bale makes a good, flat seat and an old oil drum or orange box may suffice, though a little padding is always welcome. More dedicated 'pigeon poppers' who like to shoot sitting often make their own swivel seats. Wildfowlers too sometimes get by with whatever is at hand, washed up by the tide, but the enthusiast may make a low, purpose-built model from metal tubing joining the seat to a flat base which will not sink into the mud.

Much more important is protecting one's hearing. 'Gun deafness' —permanent hearing loss (oddly, mostly in the ear furthest from the gun)—is very common among shooters. The damage is caused slowly and imperceptibly and is irreversible, so protectors should be worn as often as possible.

Ear muffs are widely accepted in clay-pigeon shooting, but they are less practical for all quarry shooting, where the ability to hear birds, beaters, dogs, and drive signals is important. They also look odd and out of place in the shooting field. Less obtrusive are ear plugs, some of which are designed so the attenuation rises as the noise level goes up. This enables the wearer to hear noises such as ordinary conversation while protecting against the worst impulsive noise. They are less efficient than muffs but you may consider this an acceptable risk if you do not shoot often. More simple, cheaper, linear ear plugs of the preformed or foam type act much like muffs. You can also get more expensive muffs whose characteristics can be varied between linear and non-linear.

All shooters who wear spectacles should have plastic rather than glass lenses as their relative lightness means they are less likely to break when dropped and they are far less likely to shatter and damage the eyes when struck. They are available with an invisible ('diamond') surface hardening which resists scratching.

Even Guns with good eyesight will gain much through owning a good pair of binoculars to scan for quarry or simply watch the wildlife. For wildfowlers and pigeon shooters studying flightlines they are essential. Most suitable are prismatic glasses of moderate magnification and with a wide field of view, such as 7×50 or 8×40. High magnification models—even ×10 or ×12—are very hard to focus without support and their usual narrow field of view makes them useless for following birds in flight.

One item I would not be without is insect repellant, the most effective I know of being 'Jungle Formula'. Without this odourless liquid, sporting after rabbits and pigeons on a warm summer's evening can be misery.

The pigeon shooter will also benefit from a good, lightweight, portable hide. Bale hides are fine on the stubbles and a few discreetly placed branches may work wonders in the hedgerow, but the ability to change positions quickly is very important. He will also welcome a face mask and a few artificial decoys, though real shot birds are generally more effective, as long as they are propped up well.

The wildfowler will also need a waterproof groundsheet for his lying pit on sand or mud, and perhaps a low hide. Other equipment that improves his safety is described in Chapter 4.

Finally, all Guns should have a proper 'priest' slipped into the pocket to despatch all wounded birds as quickly and humanely as possible. A sharp knife is useful for gutting rabbits.

## THE GAMEBOOK

An unnecessary but very desirable accessory for all quarry shooters is a gamebook. Regularly recording your bags not only enables you to help with national surveys, make useful local comparisons, and assess trends, but also provides a rich documentation of your life for you to dote over in later years, especially when it is enhanced by notes on the weather, wildlife, the land generally, and even fellow Guns.

# THE QUARRY

Long ago civilized man hunted all palatable birds and mammals as part of a wide-ranging diet. But even in the earliest civilizations certain species were reserved for royalty or other dominant members of society, and a few enjoyed total protection, often for religious reasons. With a relatively small and scattered human population, the level of hunting had little impact on quarry numbers and it was well into the nineteenth century before the age of conservation dawned. The arrival of efficient guns coincided with the first real human population explosion and immediately it was obvious that certain quarry needed legal protection. As the need for pot-hunting diminished, the concept of sport took over and increasingly restrictive legislation reduced both the number of species which could be taken and the length of open seasons. The last major review came in 1981 when the Wildlife & Countryside Act removed thirteen bird species from the quarry list. In this section I describe the wide variety of species which we can still shoot.

# GAMEBIRDS

For centuries, the sporting significance of these few species has been recognized by special legislation—now rather anachronistic. Most people are familiar with the very widespread pheasant and partridge, but few know much of the group's wilder, more local species such as ptarmigan and black grouse.

## *PHEASANT*

The pheasant is Britain's most commonly shot gamebird. A thoroughly efficient rearing-and-release programme puts about twelve to fifteen million birds into our coverts annually. The harsh, uncompromising countryside created by agricultural fanaticism since World War II cannot sustain the great numbers of indigenous grey partridges which were the lifeblood of British shooting right up to the 1930s, so now the more easily accommodated but introduced pheasant is clearly top of the bags.

On the other hand, the enormous and increasing interest in pheasant shooting has meant both continuing preservation and improvement of much habitat, fortuitously providing havens for a very wide range of threatened plants and animals. It is fair to say that producing pheasants has done more for conservation in lowland Britain than any other form of cropping or harvesting ever did.

Although pheasant shooting's importance to conservation has been significant over only the last century or so, in the wake of rapidly increasing habitat destruction, this spectacular bird has been living wild in Britain for a thousand years. It is not clear who introduced it, but we do know that it was eaten in Roman Britain, though it is unlikely that it then went feral. The earliest British record of wild-living pheasants dates from 1059 and substantial introductions were made by the Normans towards the end of the eleventh century.

These birds came from the Caucasus and became known as Old English—still a great favourite with traditionalists, but since the late eighteenth century introductions have been mostly from China, the male's white neck ring earning the common name 'ring-necked pheasant'.

Now, with rearing and release so commonplace, pheasants are found everywhere in Britain except on the highest and most inhospitable hills, and with artificial feeding can exist even where the habitat is scarcely suitable. Density is low away from areas of game preservation and the original Asian habitat along the borders of river reed beds is used little except in the East Anglian Fens, though there is a preference for well-watered country.

The British pheasant has become mainly a bird of wooded agricultural land, parkland and large estates and thrives best where woods contain a good 'bottom', with thick undergrowth adjacent to feeding fields with light soil. Optimum conditions are found in

*Previous pages* The magnificent cock pheasant: introduced from the East many centuries ago and now the nucleus of most British gameshooting.

south-eastern Britain, especially in Norfolk and Suffolk, where some estates, such as royal Sandringham, can still put up a good show of entirely wild birds through sympathetic farming and habitat control.

Areas of scrub, hedgerows, and strips of woodland are important too—far better in fact than great unbroken tracts of forest. Such habitat should provide a suitable variety of wild foods such as hedge fruit and will hold birds well when surrounding estates are largely sterile, but most shoots must resort to winter feeding of grain and sow special crops for cover as well as food.

The variety of natural foods taken is wide and ranges from the fruits, seeds, and leaves of wild plants to leatherjackets, wireworms, caterpillars, ants, grasshoppers, lizards, small birds, voles, worms, slugs, snails, and small snakes.

The mainly copper-coloured, iridescent cock is unmistakeable with his large red wattle over the eye and streaming tail of 18-24 in. At 30-35 in overall he is considerably larger than the 21-25 in, relatively dull, brown female. Wild birds are generally smaller and are said to be much better parents as well as more agile and sporting targets, but some say they lack the stamina for day-long driving. The Game Conservancy has estimated that a pheasant drains the energy reserves in its muscles in just eight seconds, then it glides.

Occasionally birds show characteristic plumage of both sexes, notably with old hens assuming cock plumage. Cocks moult in June and July and hens in July and August. Typically, he weighs 2 lb 7 oz within a range of about 1 lb 5 oz-4 lb 7 oz and she 2 lb 4 oz within a range of about 1 lb 10 oz-3 lb 9 oz.

Towards the end of March cocks crow more and fight over hens, gathering as many as possible. Their *korr-kok* or *kok-kok* calls are now among the most familiar and loved sounds of the countryside.

The cock may claim some four acres, but the hens wander about in groups behaving promiscuously: each hen's range may include the territories of four or more cocks. Pair bonds are short-lived.

Records of cocks assisting in the incubation, and even brooding, are rare. The female alone scrapes a ground hollow for a nest and lines it scantily with leaves and grass, generally among thick vegetation.

The seven to fifteen mostly pale olive-brown eggs are laid between March and September, with the peak from late April to June, though there are records from February in exceptionally mild weather.

Incubation takes twenty-three to twenty-seven days and when the hen leaves the nest voluntarily to feed for a short time she will often cover the clutch with leaves before flying from the site and later returning in the same manner—sensible precautions against the main predators, the fox, stoat, and rat.

Golden, Lady Amherst's, and Reeves' pheasants also now breed freely in the wild in parts of Britain, while in others the common pheasant has hybridized with black grouse, capercaillie, and guinea fowl.

The very sedentary pheasant spends its entire life within a few square miles, though the cock's winter range may increase by 50 per cent or more. This gregarious bird forms small parties or 'nids' and, despite semi-domestication, soon learns to run for cover or crouch till danger has passed. In fact it is loath to fly and will run swiftly ahead of beaters and dogs, but when it approaches the Guns or otherwise sees no easy escape it will rocket explosively away, vertically, if necessary, to clear the trees. It rises noisily on short, whirring wings, the strong, rapid flight being engaged only to gain sufficient height, whereupon it glides silently on decurved wings, alternately flapping and gliding before dropping into cover at the earliest opportunity. It cannot be induced to fly strongly away from its home covert and will fly fast and far to get back to it, so the day's drives must be planned accordingly and should always allow birds plenty of time to return to their favourite roosts well before dark.

A competent swimmer, the pheasant has a strong preference for roosting over water and always prefers trees with comfortable horizontal branches and warm foliage such as that of evergreens. Some adults roost on the ground in summer, but prefer a good vantage point, and juveniles do not generally take to the trees before October. They often roost in the same trees night after night and their reluctance to move on makes them an easy target for poachers.

In rearing pheasants, the great estates have advantages of large-scale production over the small producer, who would do better to buy poults from game farms rather than rear from the egg stage. Small shoots are better employed in improving the habitat to receive the birds, especially as wild birds always make much better parents and enjoy a higher survival rate. An average shoot's bag consists of about two-thirds wild birds and even in areas of heavy rearing and release about a third of the birds shot are wild. Habitat improvement also generally helps other game and wildlife.

There is a great deal of advice available today on rearing and keepering, with special courses run by organizations such as the Game Conservancy, but it is most important that the theory is adapted to local conditions. For example, on a mainly wild bird shoot, obviously the habitat must be capable of supporting whatever breeding stock is left to over-winter. There is absolutely no point in putting down vast numbers of birds on inhospitable land and expecting the wild bird population to increase.

Many shoots tag birds to study returns in the bag, but overall the average for reared pheasants on well-keepered ground is only 40 per cent. But despite its reliance on man and slowness to adapt in the many western countries where it has been introduced, the common pheasant remains a colourful and exciting part of our avifauna.

## GREY PARTRIDGE

Before the day of the pheasant the native grey or English partridge was not only Number One gamebird but also the ultimate symbol of unspoilt England and the delight of every countryman. For centuries it was always the partridge covey which featured in those charming paintings and prints of walked-up shooting, when everything proceeded at a leisurely pace. And although the bird's decline started way back in the infancy of agricultural 'efficiency', it was not really till the late 1950s that it became evident that the worldwide partridge population had tumbled to a fraction of its former level.

The ethos of the grey partridge persists in modern gameshooting circles, driving our researchers on in an attempt to reinstate the bird's cherished dominion over our traditional patchwork-quilt landscape.

The grey partridge was an ideal quarry for the old-style walk-up, though the endless going-away shots could not have taxed the average Gun too much. Today they are more likely to be encountered on driven shoots, often along with pheasants, when they can provide a wide variety of testing shots. A large proportion will have been reared and released, but many shoots, especially commercial and those in south-east England, have turned to the more easily managed and introduced French or redlegged partridge.

The main cause of the bird's decline is probably widespread use of pesticides, particularly herbicides and insecticides, which have reduced the supply of insect food available to chicks, resulting in widespread starvation. However, the number being hand-reared has increased over the last decade and this has improved the bag in southern England.

Pesticides affect many species, of course, and the fate of the grey partridge is an alarming indicator of what might have happened to many less-studied species. Fortunately, many will now benefit as the notorious grain mountains are reduced and there is growing interest in alternative land uses, with organic farming and sporting lets on the increase. Meanwhile, the grey partridge remains widespread but should be shot sparingly according to local conditions and yearly fluctuations.

The grey partridge is indeed worth caring for and boasts a remarkable natural history. It is even a world record holder in that it lays the largest single clutch of any bird—an average of fifteen to nineteen eggs in countries including Britain, rising to an average sixteen in parts of Finland. Such high production is linked to heavy mortality and always marked among ground-nesting gamebirds vulnerable to many predators.

Partridge density and nesting success are highest on farms with traditionally small fields and plenty of hedgerows and rough ground in areas of mixed farming. Monocultures and prairie farming have been particularly damaging. But a wide variety of habitats is used, including the seashore, allotments, and suburban wastes as well as pasture, heaths, commons, dunes, and brecks.

On approach, birds will sit very tight, but once up, the rufous tail is a good identification mark. In the field the sexes are not easy to identify, but the hen is less boldly marked and her breast 'horseshoe' is generally fainter than that of the male and sometimes even missing. The 12 in cock weighs 13-15 oz and the 11½ in hen 12-14 oz.

Calling partridges are sheer delight and the species has possibly the largest vocabulary of any gamebird. Its most familiar cry is the loud and harsh *kerric-kerric-kerric*, frequently uttered at dusk or well after dark by both sexes, particularly during the breeding season.

Coveys mostly break up into breeding pairs in late January or early February, though pairing has taken place in December in exceptionally mild weather. Establishing territory is very important to secure food at a lean time of year and it is not surprising that cocks become very aggressive.

Unlike the pheasant, the species is strictly monogamous and the cock is a good husband. The hen selects the nest-site in thick vegetation in April, and banks are preferred as they avoid water-logging in very wet weather. The best vegetation at the spring nest-site is long grass remaining from the previous season.

The nest scrape is lined with dried vegetation, often with a small blackberry branch or twig arched over it, apparently for protection and concealment, or shade from the sun when the leaves come out. But protection from the wind and being able to catch the sun appear to be important in site selection early in the season.

Because insect food is so important to the young, most eggs are laid in late May so that peak hatching occurs in June, to coincide with peak food availability. But the pale-olive or buff eggs are laid from late April and incubated for twenty-four days by the hen only, starting on the day the last egg is laid. The clutch is covered when the hen leaves the nest voluntarily and the cock escorts her to feed. Desertion is rare: indeed, she will even sit through thunderstorms and allow herself to be stroked on the nest.

The eggs all hatch within a few hours and the cock shelters the first chicks out under his wings until the hen is able to take over. Together, they stoutly defend their single brood, will feign injury, and even attack dogs.

Apart from insects, food includes grain, buds, the flowers and leaves of low-growing plants, spiders, slugs, and small snails, proportions varying with availability and time of year. Feeding is most intense in the early morning and evening and birds are loath to leave favourite haunts. Frequently they can be found at the same places at the same times every day, perhaps laying-up in cover during the heat of early afternoon or dust-bathing or basking.

Coveys feed and sleep together, usually roosting or 'jugging' on the ground in grass or other vegetation, generally in a rough arc, which has the advantage of making predators easier to spot.

Although habitat management remains top priority on the partridge shoot, it is certain that a change of emphasis from the old-fashioned style of keepering, in which every nest was marked and looked after, to reliance on rearing and release, has contributed to partridge decline. Indeed, releasing for restocking is not advocated, but transfer of wild birds to an area with initially very low numbers (due to poor management) may be advisable.

Very often difficulties with reared partridges arise through failure to recognize unsuitable habitats in the first place. A Game Conservancy advisory visit is always worthwhile and may save a great deal of time and money in the long run.

It is a sobering thought that to restore grey partridge numbers to their pre-1952 level would require a five- or six-fold increase.

## REDLEGGED PARTRIDGE

For a long time the introduced redlegged partridge was frowned upon by the average English sportsman, but since the demise of the grey partridge it is more widely recognized as a most valuable quarry.

This noisy bird is not native to Britain: the first recorded attempt at introduction was in 1673. Others followed before success came in Suffolk in 1790, with several thousand eggs imported from France. Hence the bird's other common name—the French partridge.

In those early days most partridges were shot walked-up and for this the numerous coveys of greys were ideal, squatting to allow close approach by Guns. But the redleg always prefers to run and is thus unsuitable for walking-up. When dogs and beaters approach, it is up and away with surprising speed. Driving is the only way to get a reasonable bag.

However, the redleg is faster on the wing than the grey partridge and offers a more sporting target, though the grey too is a very testing driven bird. Flight is easy and strong, generally taking a low line with little change of direction. More importantly, whereas coveys of greys tend to burst into view as one, redlegs tend to come over the Guns as singletons or in twos or threes. Thus Guns are less likely to be flustered and can pick their shots more deliberately, at the same time improving their kills-to-cartridges ratio. Redlegs are also useful in helping to break up driven coveys of greys.

The redleg has also gained favour because it is relatively easy to rear and release and hold on the ground, whereas released greys are notorious for their wandering.

Despite a little decline through pesticides and habitat alteration, the redleg remains widespread, though its preference is for drier land than that favoured by the grey partridge. Optimum conditions are

The grey or English partridge was Britain's most important gamebird before intensive agriculture destroyed much of its habitat and insect food.

found in East Anglia, with intensive agriculture in a Continental-type climate, low rainfall, and a light soil. Sandy heaths, coastal dunes and shingle, chalk downland, and to a lesser extent woodland rides or glades, are also frequented. It likes rougher ground than the grey, with more bush, and the heavy, wet wealden soils are always avoided, not the least because the bird's feet can become so balled-up with clay that flight is impossible.

Only small numbers exist in the wetter parts of northern and western Britain, but even there careful release schemes can be rewarding if expert advice is taken.

A great asset to building up local populations is the bird's fascinating breeding cycle—unique in Britain. The female often lays two clutches in separate nests—one for her mate to incubate and one for herself. The ten to fifteen buffish, spotted red-brown eggs are laid from late April to May and the common occurrence of large clutches—up to twenty-eight recorded—is thought to have some compensatory factor for the British climate.

Unfortunately, the high rate of egg production is offset by increased losses as, unlike the grey, the redleg never covers its eggs when left and many are destroyed by predators such as rats and stoats.

Another remarkable adaptation is the eggs' peculiar resistance to chilling and neglect. They are not usually laid on consecutive days, frequently being left for thirty-six to forty-eight hours. Surprisingly, clutches left uncovered for weeks and eventually incubated by the male are hatched as successfully as those incubated immediately.

Pairing begins in February, and the coveys break up and start breeding later and over a longer period than those of the grey, small coveys being found even into April.

Favourite nest-sites are generally hard to find in hedge bottoms, nettlebeds, or other thick cover, and for once it is the cock which makes the scantily lined scrape. Incubation takes twenty-three to twenty-five days. The chicks leave the nest and run almost as soon as hatched, are tended by both parents and fly after about fourteen days.

At long distance it is not easy to tell redleg from grey, but within shooting range the black-and-white eye stripes and barred flanks of the Frenchman may be visible. Also it lacks the grey's dark horseshoe on the breast. In the field the sexes are indistinguishable, but in the hand look for the cock's knob-like spurs. Bill, legs, and feet are coral red and the bird is slightly larger than the grey. The male's average length is 13½ in and weight 1 lb 2 oz whereas the female averages 13 in and 15½ oz.

Food is mostly vegetable and includes leaves, cereals, and seeds as well as insects and spiders. In common with other gamebirds, the young are dependent on the extra protein derived from animal food for rapid growth during the first few weeks of life. Fortunately, the young are better at ranging than those of the grey partridge and occasionally get by on certain plant foods without many insects.

The Frenchman is a bold bird and often sits nonchalantly on fences and walls along country roads while cars whizz past. It likes a perch with a commanding view and will even sit in trees. In roosting it favours off-ground sites, frequently bunching tight in a tree.

The bird's calling also often brings it to attention, especially in spring. The cock's repertoire is long and varied, with a distinctive, loud and challenging *chucka chucka* or *chuck-chuck-ar*. Birds that are put up often cry *kuk kuk* and a shrill, treble *crik-ik-ik* is also common.

## RED GROUSE

The red grouse is regarded as the most challenging and exciting of our main gamebirds by the great majority of shooters who have been lucky enough to try the range. Equally importantly, the species is the prime reason for the retention of vast acreages of British moorland, an outstandingly beautiful habitat which supports much wildlife of significant rarity and restricted range and is cherished by sportsmen and conservationists alike.

The ups and downs of grouse stocks remain a perennial topic of sporting conversation. No one can deny the cyclical nature of grouse populations but disagreement remains as to the best course of action to arrest protracted decline in many areas.

The red grouse is a thoroughly wild bird and, unlike the pheasant and partridge, it is not a suitable subject for widespread rearing and release, mostly because of its reliance on heather for food and the difficulty of changing from an artificial to a natural diet. Thus the emphasis must remain on habitat management, but at least this ensures continuance of the bird's attractive wildness. A wild bird in a wild, inspirational setting: what more could one ask?

For many years the red grouse was regarded as the only bird species entirely restricted to the British Isles, but now it is classed merely as a well-marked island subspecies (race) of the willow grouse which ranges across America and Eurasia. Whereas the willow grouse has white wings all year, our red grouse has no need to change to winter-white in a milder climate.

Red grouse are subject to considerable plumage variation, especially regionally. For example, Irish birds are generally paler. In addition, both male and female have two distinct moults each year, but the male's are in autumn and winter whereas the female's are in summer and autumn.

The cock's comb is large and red whereas the hen's is smaller and pinker. She is paler and more heavily barred with lighter pigment, whereas he has thinner, more wavy lines and spots. The hen usually has more brown and yellow mottling on the wings and dark tail. Adults appear greyer in winter with white underwing-coverts, and occasionally show white on the flanks and belly. Legs are feathered down to the claws. The average cock measures 14-15½ in and weighs 1 lb 8 oz and the hen 13-14 in and 1 lb 4½ oz.

Basically, grouse are found where the heather is, chiefly in northern Britain. Most moors are at 975-1,950 ft, but heather occurs at different heights in different areas and in parts of Scotland goes right down to sea level. The traditional stronghold has been the Scottish Highlands, but the area has seen some of the worst decline in recent years. There are also significant populations on Orkney, the Outer Hebrides, the Border hills, parts of the Lake District, the Yorkshire Moors, Northumberland, and the Pennines, northern England providing some of the best sport. Wales has lost most of its best moors to forestry in recent times and in southern England there have been only tiny relict populations on Dartmoor and Exmoor.

Good moor management is the key to high grouse density, involving traditional control of predators, especially foxes and crows, and above all rotational burning to ensure a continuous succession of young heather shoots for food. Burning also keeps down the tick population which spreads disease, but some old heather must be left for shelter and nesting.

Early concern over grouse decline concentrated on disease, particularly strongylosis. Known for 200 years, this is quite natural, but under intense grouse management, when the stock is too high, epidemics occur. Shooting reduces the disease by reducing the stock.

The local population limit is determined by the moor's underlying rock, grouse densities being highest over base-rich rocks which increase soil fertility and therefore the nutritional value of the heather. Application of fertilizers, provision of grit, and drainage of waterlogged areas can also be important.

Overgrazing by sheep, deer and cattle has been a major problem, allowing in useless, rank grasses where heather has been eaten right out. However, it has been demonstrated conclusively that the major reason for grouse decline is deterioration of heather quality brought about by a reduction in the number of keepers. Much of the endless, esoteric research seems to be largely a waste of time and, providing the climate is reasonable, there would appear to be no better way to achieve consistently good bag returns than religiously attending to the above points and carefully planning shooting according to production. Many problems have arisen through over-shooting linked to increasing commercialism.

The red grouse feeds almost entirely on ling heather, especially in winter, eating the shoots, flowers, and seed heads, adults preferring the current year's growth from plants aged about three years. Back-up foods include stalks and leaves of bilberry, shoots and fruits of cranberry, flowers and shoots of moss crop, bog myrtle, dwarf willow, grass, rushes, clover and bracken, birch buds, and catkins.

Insects are important to the chicks in their first two weeks, but not to the same extent as for young partridges, for whom wet summers can be disastrous. Fortunately, heather dries quickly. Grouse chicks also eat heather tips, moss capsules, and various flowers from the first day. After ten days plant food dominates and at three weeks the diet is entirely adult.

The species is generally monogamous, but a male with a large territory may hold two hens which both nest within his patch. Cocks spar from autumn and in a mild winter pairing occurs from December. Territories may be taken as early as October.

The hen makes a simple scrape in the ground, lined with grass and heather, in which she lays six to eleven (occasionally four to seventeen) creamy-white eggs, almost obscured by chocolate-red blotches, from late April into May. The twenty-two to twenty-four day incubation is by the hen.

Chicks leave the nest soon after hatching and the single brood is tended by both sexes. They can flutter at seven days and fly at twelve to eighteen, but remain together as a family into autumn, as late as November. A lost clutch is usually replaced by a second, smaller one.

After a few days shooting in an early season, coveys start to pack and by the end of August they are already more wary and wild. Then in September and October getting good bags is more difficult, with so many holding together and tending to pass the butts as one.

Grouse without territories are driven into marginal areas where, progressively weakened through hunger and exposed to predators, they soon die. They are non-dispersive (80-90 per cent die within about a mile of where ringed) so the surplus fails to move to other moors and is eliminated by April. Thus in all years the aim is to shoot hard and early to bag as many of the reckoned surplus as possible (obviously leaving sufficient breeding stock) before packing makes them more difficult to shoot. They will die anyway. Grouse are short-lived birds. Nearly two out of three alive in August die within a year, irrespective of shooting.

With the right dogs, grouse also provide excellent walked-up shooting, which is far cheaper than most driven sport. Bags are inevitably small but Guns return year after year to savour the glorious world of the grouse.

## BLACK GROUSE

This handsome bird has suffered great range contraction over the last 200 years as much of its favoured marginal habitat has been destroyed, especially in southern England, where land development hit first. Most English counties lost their blackgame in the late nineteenth and early twentieth centuries.

Blackgame are most common along woodland fringes. They are also found on open moorland dominated by heather, generally with a few trees and scrub nearby. Also favoured are swampy areas with bogs and rushes, streams, and ponds. Conifer plantations up to about twenty years old are frequented, but so too are mature, open pine forests with heavy undergrowth, along with open birch woods. High rocks are sometimes resorted to for shelter. Birds venture from these rough areas to feed on adjacent marginal agricultural land and in autumn tall bracken is favoured, especially when next to stubbles.

A few pairs remain on the Quantocks and Exmoor, but generally the bird does not breed in England south of Staffordshire. Wales has modest numbers but Scotland has a good surplus, the stronghold being in the hilly districts of the west and north.

Most of the many introduction and reintroduction attempts have failed, including those to Ireland, where the species is not native. However, there is a current introduction attempt in Ireland. As always, the main problems are maintaining large enough areas of suitable habitat and minimizing disturbance. But there appears to have been a recent increase in some areas, largely through greatly extended young afforestation, though this may merely be more efficient recording.

Abroad, the blackcock is sought after as a sporting trophy, though the practice of spring shooting with rifles is decreasing. Even in Britain there is an undoubted emphasis on the cock, which regrettably is more often valued for its fine feathers than superb sporting qualities.

Driven shooters have been frustrated by the black grouse as it is such an unpredictable, strong-willed bird which will not follow pattern in the manner of pheasant, partridge, and even red grouse. Whereas red grouse do not seem to mind flying downwind, blackgame avoid it, perhaps because of the cock's lyre-shaped tail.

Driving blackgame is very difficult indeed as when they are put up their direction is uncertain. Flushed birds often circle and return whence they came or simply double back over the beaters. Thus a Gun walking in the line often enjoys good sport. Flankers are often ineffective in dissuading the birds from flying out the sides of a drive.

Blackgame are also reluctant to fly uphill and when flushed on a slope will often slip away to a lower level. Any shot at generally rise high and fast, frequently leaving the area entirely and denying neighbouring Guns the chance of a shot. Thus commercial blackgame shooting is very unpredictable.

However, anyone prepared to tramp after the blackcock in his wild haunts will find grand sport. The 21-in bird rises quite unexpectedly and almost silently into powerful, rapid flight and, as with capercaillie and geese, do not be deceived by its bulk (2 lb 5 oz-3 lb 14 oz): it is often faster than driven grouse! The female (the greyhen) is no less sporting, though considerably smaller at 16-17 in and weighing 1 lb 10½ oz-2 lb 7 oz.

Blackgame have a spectacular courtship ceremony at favoured sites called leks. There the cocks arrive in March to joust: mostly sham fighting with a great deal of hopping up and down and tails fanned. Sometimes feathers fly as individuals try to reach the lek centre, which is the best place to secure matings. However, the species is not truly polygamous, but rather promiscuous, and the cock does not leave the lek with a harem. He only mates there.

In fact the cock is a poor father and takes no part in nesting duties.

The hen makes a scrape beneath a bush or among other vegetation and lines it with a few leaves and a little grass. Some nests are on the open moor or, exceptionally, in the tree nest of another species.

The six to ten buff, sparsely spotted red-brown eggs are laid from late April into June and incubated by the greyhen alone for twenty-four to twenty-seven days. Chicks leave the nest soon after hatching, are tended by the greyhen alone, and can fly after about twenty-one days, though they are not fully grown till much later. They stay with the hen till autumn approaches but young cocks often form packs by mid-August. Productivity can be extremely low in a wet season, when nests are frequently washed away.

Almost entirely vegetarian, the black grouse can damage forestry through eating young tree shoots, causing the development of 'stag heads'. But overall conifer feed forms only a small part of the diet and economic losses occur only locally. Tree nurseries should be sited well away from blackgame concentrations and special care taken when heavy snow denies the birds their usual diet.

Heather is important, especially in winter, but blackgame are much more omnivorous than red grouse and take seeds, ground fruits, and the buds and shoots of many plants and trees.

The hen usually prefers to roost on the ground in summer, but the cock spends much of his time in trees and always prefers to roost aloft, except during his July/August moult. They may huddle together in trees during a severe snowstorm and sometimes burrow into a drift for shelter.

The black grouse is a magical quarry, a bird of wild places, and we must hope that more enlightened forestry and conservation interests allow it more space to spread its wings in the future.

## CAPERCAILLIE

Britain's biggest gamebird, the capercaillie, is a member of the grouse family and it is no less sporting than its renowned relatives. The turkey-sized cock averages 33-36 in long and weighs 7 lb 8 oz-9 lb 11 oz, but much larger birds are said to have occurred. Because of this great bulk the bird's flight is very deceptive and this might well be the most difficult shot of all our gamebirds.

Actually, the 'wood grouse' is not legally a gamebird and you do not need a game licence to shoot it because when the Game Act of 1831 was passed the species had become extinct in Britain. It died out in England around 1670, but was still common in Scotland and Ireland at the end of the seventeenth century, before widespread felling of natural pine forest sealed its fate. The last-known indigenous Scottish stock was shot on Deeside in 1785 and the Irish population terminated in about 1790.

Obviously the bird's conspicuousness helped to bring about its downfall through shooting and snaring, yet it was sporting interest which prompted reintroduction, with Swedish birds in the 1830s.

Today's stock is entirely descended from introduced birds.

With the accent on trophy taking abroad, it is not surprising that Continental Guns pay large sums to shoot Scottish cock capers. This has pressurized the British stock, but fortunately the population is thriving through increased afforestation this century.

Unfortunately, reintroductions to England and Ireland have generally failed, but there is every reason to hope that the magnificent caper will again find a clawhold in Britain outside Scotland. It is now found throughout the Highlands, especially east and central, but it finds difficulty in establishing permanent breeding haunts in the wetter west.

The caper's favourite habitat is old, natural woods of Scots pine with open glades, but little of this remains. Fortunately it is one of a small number of relatively uncommon species which have taken to the new, northern coniferous forests, especially in hilly areas. Pine plantations are first colonized at fifteen to twenty years old and larch and spruce at twenty to thirty years old, especially when mixed with Scots pine. But the birds are often seen on heather and in stubble fields well away from woods.

However, the caper's diet does bring the bird into conflict with forestry interests. In winter and early spring it feeds almost exclusively on the needles, and to a lesser extent the buds, shoots, cones and seeds, of Scots pine, larch and Douglas fir. The birds concentrate on pines after the first snows have fallen, generally in November, and most damage is done when the bursting buds and new shoots are eaten. Healthy trees may recover but thin, straggling plantations may be seriously affected. Nursery trees next to established forest seem to be particularly vulnerable because they are so conspicuous and they may have increased nutritive value through the addition of fertilizers.

Because of the great difference in size between the male and female (average 23-25 in long, weighing 3lb 5 oz-4 lb 5oz), the sexes have different preferences in winter feeding habits, so much so that flocks of males and females remain completely segregated. Females prefer lower branches, where they have more protection from predators, whereas the cocks feed confidently in crowns of trees. But despite all their cunning the birds lose weight in midwinter as the feeding day is not long enough to sustain their bulk with relatively low-energy foods.

In spring and summer a much wider range of foods is taken, including berries, grass, leaves and buds of birch, alder, hazel, and animal foods such as ants and their eggs, beetles and worms. The young need extra animal food to get sufficient protein for growth.

As with blackgame, the male's extraordinary displays take place on special grounds called leks, but again the species is promiscuous rather than polygamous. Some exceptionally bold cocks will even defend their territories against men and dogs.

The magnificent cock capercaillie – Britain's biggest gamebird – is surprisingly fast in flight.

The hen makes a scrape in the ground, often at the foot of a large pine tree, and lines it with vegetation. More unusual sites are in open heather or other low shrubs and in the tree nests of other species.

The single clutch of five to eight pale-yellow, speckled-brown eggs is laid from late April into May and incubated by the hen alone for twenty-six to twenty-nine days. The chicks leave the nest within hours of hatching, are tended by the hen only and can flutter after two or three weeks, though they are not fully grown until much later.

The huge, generally black male with feathered legs and shaggy 'beard' cannot be confused with any other British bird, even in flight, when the long, broad wings and square-ended tail can make the bird appear even larger. However, the smaller, mottled, ruddy-brown female could be confused with the greyhen, but the reddish patch on her breast should distinguish.

There have been many hybrids between blackcock and female capercaillie and between pheasant and capercaillie. These mostly occur in areas of range expansion, where the female capers usually arrive first, and in the absence of cocks of their own species mate with black grouse or pheasant.

Any opportunity to shoot driven caper should be welcomed, but Guns will need to be on their toes, even when the birds occasionally get up noisily from the ground and give plenty of warning of their approach. Those taking off from trees are much quieter and can easily sweep past almost undetected with a series of rapid wingbeats alternating with long glides, the neck extended, weaving easily through the trees.

Sportsmen seeking caper in winter will find them mostly in trees – feeding, sitting to digest meals and roosting. Most summer roosts, too, are in trees, the same being used night after night. Birds in open areas are said to burrow into snow for shelter and to roost.

Though secure, the British population is thought to number less than ten thousand pairs and it is to be hoped that foresters will recognize the species' sporting potential. For their part, sportsmen should restrict themselves to very modest bags and ensure that the pull of commercialism never results in over-shooting and excessive disturbance. Optimum habitat may yield seventeen to twenty birds per square kilometre, but areas of range expansion will have very low densities and obviously potential colonisers should not be shot.

The cock caper is one of the greatest spectacles of British woodland. Its curious calls include sounds like cork-popping, rattling and knife-grinding and can easily convince the unsuspecting that goblins are abroad. But the visiting sportsman will not hear this incredible vocal range as the caper is mostly silent outside the breeding season.

80

## *PTARMIGAN*

Only the keenest sportsmen venture after the ptarmigan, which is superbly adapted to life at high altitude and is most famous for changing its camouflage to suit each season. But despite the wildness and remoteness of its habitat, this is yet another species which has suffered great range contraction, chiefly at the hand of man, and was already virtually extinct in England and Wales by 1800. Now in Britain it is confined to Scotland.

Much of its plant food was grazed right out by introduced sheep and isolated groups were unable to maintain viable numbers. Warming of the climate over the first half of this century aggravated the situation, but since the late 1950s generally lower temperatures have accompanied some increase. Armies of skiers, climbers, ramblers, and birdwatchers have invaded ptarmigan country, in parts of which the birds have become quite tame, but there is no real evidence that human presence alone is having a significant adverse effect. In fact, the areas around the ski-lifts at Cairngorm and Cairnwell provide particularly good ptarmigan spotting. Habitat destruction and alteration are the bird's worst enemies.

Scotland provides a particularly favourable habitat, ptarmigan densities being much lower in the Subarctic and Arctic. The 'white grouse' occurs from Scandinavia and Iceland across northern Eurasia to North America and Greenland. South of this northern range it occurs only on the higher parts of the Alps, the Pyrenees, central Asia, and Japan.

British birds are confined to areas of arctic-alpine heath, but the height of this varies with latitude, being much lower in north and north-west Scotland than in the Cairngorms and Grampians of the central Highlands. In these areas winter takes hold early and, although the ptarmigan-shooting season is early too—12 August to 10 December—reaching the ground is often more of a problem than finding the birds. Snow and ice often besiege ptarmigan territory from the end of October, and even before that mist-shrouded peaks can make shooting unsafe. Thus the visitor is advised to have several days available, especially if a long trip is necessary.

Despite their hardiness, ptarmigan do seek out the sheltered, lower corries when it is stormy, and when the sun shines they are often found basking in the lee of the wind. But with their cryptic colouring they are always hard to spot, sometimes looking like a dark stone or shadowy bump in the snow. They are always reluctant to fly in this very open country where natural predators such as eagles have a clear view, but your ranging dog must always remain very close as, once up, the birds are as fast as their cousins. With whirring flight and rapid wingbeats, alternating with glides on arched pinions, they skim swiftly away over the next brow, taking full advantage of protecting contours.

Identification of ptarmigan is not a problem for they are usually the only large birds present, and where they do overlap with red grouse can always be distinguished by their permanently white wings and underparts. The male's April to July breeding plumage is mostly dark grey and the female's buff, mottled, and barred orange-brown. He turns pale grey from August to October and the female's sandy grey is also a fitting autumnal tint. But in their November to March winter dress both birds are all white, only the tail remaining black, though even this is scarcely visible with its white tip. This third moult appears to be triggered by temperature change and is subject to considerable time variation. Therefore anyone wanting to take home a pure-white bird for mounting as a trophy is advised to delay shooting till November or December.

Both sexes have the red wattle, but the male's is much bigger and he may also be distinguished by the black mark between beak and eye. The thick feathering on feet and legs is said to assist walking on the snow, but these 'gaiters' are moulted and renewed and the claws shed (as in red grouse) between early June and the end of September. Ptarmigan weigh a little less than red grouse and have an average length of 13-14 in.

Summer is very short in ptarmigan country and the birds have time to raise only one brood. Indeed, the bird's breeding programme is superbly adapted to life on the tops: its ten-day fledging period is the quickest of any British ground-nesting bird.

Lined with a few grasses and feathers, the nest hollow is generally hidden among dwarf vegetation and is extremely hard to find as the hen sits very tight. In a favourable year the five to ten (occasionally three to twelve) creamy-white eggs with dark-brown markings are laid in early May, but not till late May or June during inclement weather. Incubation, by the female only, takes about twenty-five days. Lost clutches may be replaced as late as July.

Chicks leave the nest very soon after hatching and are usually tended by both parents for a few days only before the male deserts, though he may rejoin them later. After fledging, the young often remain with the female and join flocks from November, but some disperse as early as August. Large packs rarely occur before the end of November. With such unpredictable weather at high altitude, snowstorms and heavy rain being common even in June, chick mortality can be very high.

There is no wide variety of food above the treeline, but usually there is an abundance of heather, crowberry, and bilberry, which together form the bulk of the diet. Other mountain plants and a few insects are also taken, along with grit and the occasional drink. In severe weather ptarmigan rarely abandon the tops and when necessary will burrow into the snow for food. They often work down the mountainside, feeding early in the morning.

Because of the nature of the habitat, the population level is very hard to determine, but various estimates suggest 10,000-100,000 pairs and the autumn count may be ten times that of spring. Good numbers are found in Ross-shire, Inverness-shire, Sutherland, Banffshire, and Perthshire, but the highest recorded density is from Aberdeenshire.

This is never a bird of big bags and most sportsmen are content with a brace here and there, and visitors from afar are mostly delighted with a single trophy. However, if the strange, low croaking and grunting *kuh-kuh-kurrrrr* of the 'snowbird' is still to be heard in a hundred years' time, we must guard against excessive commercial shooting as more and more people discover British sport. Without the ptarmigan's evocative call, only the wind will be left to break the peculiar silence which broods over much of rooftop Britain.

# WADERS

Earlier this century, market gunners shot a very wide variety of waders, most of which were eaten by all sections of society. With the change to sport shooting interest in these species faded away and very few Guns complained when protection was widened in 1981. Now only three wader species may be shot throughout Britain, though the curlew and Jack snipe remain legal quarry in Northern Ireland.

Well-known for changing its plumage to suit each season, the ptarmigan is sought by only the hardiest hunters.

## WOODCOCK

In gameshooting circles the woodcock is unrivalled. It is the one bird which everyone wants to shoot, but nailing it can demand considerable prowess.

The woodcock also makes a superb meal, traditionally being roasted on toast with the 'trail' (entrails) still in, as with snipe, though this bizarre treatment is unnecessary to make the dish outstanding. And when pot-hunting was more important than sport, the woodcock was taken by whatever means were available: nets, traps, nooses, and 'springes' placed in its regular night haunts.

Today most woodcock are shot fortuitously on pheasant drives and it is absurd that the woodcock-shooting season ends on 31 January as many are shot by Guns on 1 February, the last day of the pheasant-shooting season, thereby breaking the law.

Woodcock run ahead of the line, but when the beaters and dogs are right on top of them the longbills rise swiftly with a great swish of pinions, the rather short wings lending great manoeuvrability as they weave easily through the trees, causing great excitement among the Guns. But the flight is not particularly fast and in the open the woodcock is much easier to shoot.

Undisturbed flight is even slower, though wavering, indecisive, and bat-like, and tends to follow regular flightlines at dusk. Even flushed birds are often very predictable, with paths between certain trees and other landmarks favoured in old haunts, making special woodcock drives possible where numbers permit. But their alertness and flying skills are considerable and they can disappear frustratingly, dropping into cover with remarkable suddenness.

Breeding birds need open deciduous woodland with dry ground for nesting and nearby wet or damp areas for feeding. Constantly wet or draughty woods (especially beech) with little 'bottom' are avoided, a good understorey of bracken, rhododendron, bramble, laurel, and holly being preferred. Mature coniferous woods are avoided, but young plantations with wide, grassy rides and other open spaces are used increasingly. Indeed, they are thought to have contributed significantly to recent population increase.

However, the woodcock is notoriously unpredictable and may turn up almost anywhere. The resident population is greatly outnumbered by passage migrants and winter visitors in many areas and all are subject to a considerable amount of weather-related movement as drought and frost prevent the longbill from probing for its 90 per cent earthworm diet. Thus a 'fall' of 'cock should be taken advantage of promptly, for in irregular haunts the birds are likely to have vanished within a day or two. However, walked-up birds do not usually fly far before dropping into cover.

By the mid-1930s the woodcock had been recorded breeding in every county in the British Isles, though records are few from some areas, especially in the far west, where it is too damp. It is thought that management of estates for pheasants helped great range expansion in the nineteenth and early twentieth centuries.

In winter the species is much more widespread, immigrants tending to concentrate in the mild, wet areas of the south and west, where feeding is easier. In particular, big bags have been made in the west of Ireland and south-west Cornwall. Also productive are Norfolk, through which many of the immigrants pass, and the Inner Hebrides.

Passage migrants and winter visitors from Scandinavia, Russia, and Germany start to arrive on the east coast in September, the peak influx being at the end of October and the beginning of November and the tail end in early December. Most arrive singly, though occasionally in waves owing to bad weather delaying their departure, which allows numbers to accumulate.

Immigrants often arrive exhausted and thin. Reluctant to fly, they give a false impression of tameness as they seek refuge in coastal ditches and dykes. No true sportsman would knowingly shoot them in such emaciated condition, irrespective of whether or not a severe-weather shooting suspension has been enforced. During prolonged, severe frost all 'cock move to lower, warmer ground with marshes and springs which rarely freeze, and if necessary will return to brackish marsh.

Most migrants return home in March and April, according to how far they have to travel. From March to July 'cock perform their strange 'roding' flights along regular flightpaths, with slow, owl-like wingbeats and weird calls—a few grunting croaks followed by a sharp *tsiwick* repeated several times and audible for considerable distances. This is the male's invitation for the female to call him down to copulate. He may mate with several females during a season and does not hold a territory.

The nest is very hard to find, being a mere hollow lined with dead leaves, frequently among dead bracken or light vegetation such as bramble. The four (occasionally three or five) eggs are as well camouflaged as the sitting adult, having a grey-white to brown background heavily marked with chestnut and ash-grey blotches.

Peak laying is from mid-March to mid-April and the female incubates alone for twenty to twenty-three days from the laying of the last egg, the interval between the laying of each egg being up to four days. There are usually two broods.

The downy chicks leave the nest immediately on hatching and are probably fed by the parent for a few days. To escape danger or surmount obstacles, the parent may fly for a few yards with a single chick (or even one as much as three-quarters grown) between its thighs, apparently using the depressed, fanned tail for further support.

Woodcock generally roost by day, skulking under hollies or other evergreens, and feed by night, though they also feed by day in severe frost. Lunar rhythm is thought to influence prey activity so feeding may be more intense during a full moon. And with the emphasis on earthworms, drought too can be a problem. Other foods taken include spiders, beetles, millipedes, centipedes, insects and their larvae, small freshwater molluscs, and some grass and seeds. The flight between roost and feeding ground mostly follows a regular route but if the site is close the 'cock usually walks. Although feeding grounds may be communal, the species is very unsociable and birds usually flight singly.

The species is easy to identify by its broad, rounded wings, dumpy appearance, and long bill held downwards in flight. The sexes are alike but there is considerable plumage variation. There are two main types: one mostly rufous-brown patterned black, chestnut, buff and grey; the other, rarer variety being darker and greyer. Size and weight also vary considerably, the average length being 13½ in and weight 11 oz for the male and 12 oz the female. An increasing number of 'short-billed' 'cock are being recorded but this may be linked to wider publicity and interest in such phenomena.

Men have always been proud of bagging the 'cock and today continue the tradition of displaying its 'pin feathers' in their hat-bands, as symbols of sporting prowess. The 'pin' is the small, pointed, narrow feather at the root of the wing's first primary and because of its elasticity was once sought after by painters, who used it for fine 'pen' work.

### COMMON SNIPE

Snipe have been cooked in British kitchens as long as we have had powder and shot, and before that they were trapped, but whereas medieval banquets seem to have had an inexhaustible supply, continual land drainage since then means that the little longbill is increasingly a gourmet's treat. There was some increase and colonization of southern English counties earlier this century, but this appears to have been a temporary phenomenon linked to climatic change. Fortunately, upland strongholds have fared much better, largely through their inaccessibility and unsuitability for farming or other development. However, increased afforestation of bog and moorland brings a new threat to the snipe and many other species through habitat loss.

The snipe is one of Britain's most testing quarry. The female incubates alone for eighteen to twenty days.

Nonetheless, the common snipe is still very widespread in Britain, with probably at least 100,000 breeding pairs augmented by many visitors. The greatest concentrations of breeding birds are on the damp moors of northern Scotland and Ireland. Most resident snipe make only local, weather-related movements from their damp inland haunts to feed on the shore, but in severe frost will range much wider, some migrating to western Europe. At least a few passage migrants and winter visitors turn up in most areas.

Ideally, the snipe likes clear, boggy patches for feeding, alongside reeds or other long vegetation in which to rest or hide. It must have wet ground such as water meadows, rushy fields, saltmarsh, blanket bogs, river valleys, washes, and lake margins. Even damp corners of farm fields often attract a few, some suprisingly regularly, as do wide, damp ditches and dykes, even on otherwise barren farms.

A few places in western Britain and Ireland still find driving snipe worthwhile, and this certainly provides very exciting and testing sport. However, by far the majority of snipe are shot walked-up or flighted along with duck. They are extremely alert birds, with good eyesight and hearing, and are seen in the open far less frequently than other waders.

In walking-up snipe, the gun must be held forward at the ready as the springing birds provide little opportunity to get a shot off. Approached birds almost always crouch, unseen in reedbeds or superbly camouflaged in other vegetation, and do not fly till the last possible moment. Then they make off rapidly.

This evasiveness has long given rise to much discussion among sportsmen on the best way to approach snipe. Some insist on walking them up downwind, maintaining that, like most birds, the snipe will rise into the wind if possible and then may pass the Gun. Others prefer to approach into the wind, suggesting that this defeats the snipe's keen hearing. Whatever the method, attention must be paid to the nature of the terrain, remembering that snipe prefer to feed and rest out of the wind. Most snipe are shot going away and as a result a great many are missed underneath.

Dusk-flighting snipe is no less easy. To begin with, there is the problem of selecting shot size when hoping to shoot duck at the same time. Sizes seven and eight are most popular for snipe, but four and five more suitable for duck. Snipe usually arrive at inland waters very late, when it is almost dark, and then they are fond of dropping in suddenly from considerable height. Thus the snipe-shooter must have extremely good eyesight and swift reactions.

Reasonably easy to recognize, the snipe has a very long, straight bill over two and a half times the length of its head. The white outer tail feathers, fast zig-zag flight, and distinctive, loud, harsh *scaap* call also help to distinguish. The sexes are alike, having excellent

camouflage—stripes and bars of buff and brown, a striped head, and a very noticeable creamy double v on the back. Average length is 10½ in, including the 2¾ in bill, and average weight just 4 oz.

The simple nest hollow among sedges, rushes, or grasses is usually lined with grasses and near water. Most clutches of the four (sometimes three) pear-shaped, olive-grey or olive-brown eggs, heavily blotched with dark sepia, are laid in April, but with a very long breeding season hatching is almost continuous from May to mid-August. The female incubates alone for eighteen to twenty days.

In common with other ground-nesting birds, the chicks leave the nest within a few hours. They are tended by both parents and fly after about twenty-one days. However, it is some seven weeks before they attain the wing-length and weight of the adult. Thus in an average year there will be many immature birds from later broods to avoid at the start of the shooting season—12 August (Northern Ireland 1 October, Irish Republic 1 September).

As with some other lowland waders, snipe parents often divide the brood soon after hatching and go separate ways, each group feeding and roosting apart to reduce the risk of total brood loss to predators. Sometimes a pair has two broods in a season. Snipe are good parents and will feign injury to lead predators away from young and occasionally carry chicks, in the manner of woodcock.

Snipe feed mostly at night and roost by day in a 'form', a simple depression in long grass or other vegetation. There is an intense period of activity at dusk, when the snipe-shooter has his best flighting opportunities.

The long bill has a flexible, sensitive tip and is ideal for probing in mud and soft earth for the main diet of worms. Snipe often feed in almost liquid mud, swallowing without withdrawing the bill. Other foods include fly grubs, woodlice, water beetles, caddis larvae, snails and other molluscs, crustaceans, berries, and some seeds.

In cold weather snipe lose condition rapidly despite vigorous feeding (it is one of the species subject to severe-weather shooting suspensions) and are forced to feed more freely in the open and in daylight. During periods of full moon they feed more solidly by night and sleep more by day, probably because lunar 'rhythm' affects prey activity. They also feed when the moon is overcast.

The snipe is also well-known for its 'drumming', but this has nothing to do with voice. The resonant, quavering humming is produced mechanically by the two outer tail feathers vibrating in the wind as the bird dives steeply with the tail fanned. The note's undulation is caused by the wingbeats. Although heard mostly during courtship, especially March to mid-June, this sound is heard at any time of year and creates a pleasant air of mystery for hunters of the 'heather bleater'.

## GOLDEN PLOVER

This beautiful bird provides both superb sport and a delicious meal. Apart from woodcock and common snipe, the shooting of which requires a game licence, the golden plover is the only wader on the British quarry list since the Wildlife and Countryside Act 1981, but the Jack snipe and curlew may still be shot in Northern Ireland.

Though still one of the most abundant waders wintering in the British Isles, the bird has suffered through afforestation of upland breeding haunts and climatic amelioration this century, its range retreating northwards. Northern Scotland remains our most important breeding stronghold, though even there decline is marked. In western Ireland and northern Scotland it breeds down to sea level but in southern Britain it breeds only on land above about 4,225 ft. Almost all British birds breed on the flat or gently sloping moorland of the North and West.

The single clutch of four (occasionally three) eggs is laid mid-April to June and incubated mostly by the female for twenty-eight to thirty days. The young fly at about four weeks.

Home-bred birds are joined by large numbers of passage migrants and winter visitors in September and October, notably on the east coast. Our largest midwinter populations are in northern England, south-west England, East Anglia, southern Scotland, and Northern Ireland and most large assemblies are on or close to the coast. In hard winters birds concentrate in milder areas such as the south-west, or on any coast where the intertidal zone is free of ice.

In summer the 'goldie' is easy to identify with its black face and underparts and spangled black and gold upperparts, but shooters should be cautious as the winter plumage is much more sombre. The black disappears but the largely white underparts and pale underwing contrast well with the still yellow-flecked brownish upperparts. The compact shape, short bill, and relatively large, rounded head help to distinguish. The sexes are alike and average length is 11 in. When the shooting season opens in September a few birds may still be in almost full summer plumage.

This omnivorous species takes a wide variety of plant and animal foods, including worms, insects, spiders, small shellfish, grass and weed seeds, berries, algae, and moss. On farmland permanent pasture is a great attraction, where soil invertebrates are taken at or very near the surface. Cultivated land (especially winter-sown cereals) is used extensively in some areas, such as East Anglia, and in southern Britain arable farmland is used more heavily in winter.

Much food is taken at night, especially by moonlight, and most winter feeding is on the saltings and mudflats, though the birds frequently retire inland between tides to sleep and rest until the mudflats are exposed again. Local knowledge of this flighting routine can lead to excellent shooting.

The golden plover's flight is always fast and graceful, with very regular, rapid wingbeats, the wings slightly depressed and taking a low line. Flocks often perform spectacular aerial manoeuvres and at evening flight some really testing shooting is to be had when the birds seem almost to fall out of the sky from compact groups over the fields, to skim very low over the shoreline, rising and falling with the contours.

Better chances are to be had at dawn when there are defined flights as birds go inland, returning to the saltings soon after dusk. However, they tend to stay inland on moonlit nights. In some places tide flighting provides good sporting opportunities.

In southern Britain roosts are mainly on cultivated land, especially plough, whereas in the north grassland and coastal roosts are more popular.

With days of market gunning long past, only small numbers of golden plover are now shot, but what a sporting treasure this remains. Its plaintive call is the delight of wildfowlers everywhere, a last link with the wilderness marshes of medieval Britain.

# DUCK AND GEESE

As most are migratory and concentrate on our wilder coasts and inland marshes, duck and geese provide some of the most exciting and unpredictable quarry shooting in Britain. Their behaviour demands a lifetime's study and of necessity the successful wildfowler is an enthusiastic naturalist.

## *MALLARD*

Of the nine species of duck still on the British quarry list the mallard or 'wild duck' is by far the most familiar and the most commonly shot. Easy to rear and release, the mallard commonly vies with starlings, sparrows, and pigeons for our picnic scraps in the park or along the river, yet this same species provides superb sport in some of our wildest places. Although the ancestor of most domestic duck throughout western Europe, the wild mallard retains its great cunning and flying skills.

The mallard is found throughout the British Isles, except on the highest and most barren hills, and is our most widely distributed species of wildfowl in both summer and winter, though density varies considerably. Almost every lowland, wetland habitat is used through-out the year, as well as coasts outside the breeding season.

With its glossy green head and neck, dark breast, and white-bordered blue wing-bar (speculum), the drake is easy to identify in good light, but in the dim conditions of dawn and dusk it can be confused with protected species such as the redbreasted merganser. As with all the wildfowl, familiarity with flight pattern, silhouette, and calls will aid rapid identification.

Like most females of the family, the duck mallard is a little harder to identify. She is slightly larger than the female pintail, wigeon, shoveler, and gadwall, all of which she resembles, but in good light may be identified by her white-bordered, glossy blue speculum. In bad light her frequent quacking in flight will aid identification. Indeed, it is relatively easy to imitate the call to attract the bird within range. But the drake does not make the loud quacking like a farmyard duck. His call is softer and higher-pitched —*quork* or *quek* or *queek*, though he also utters a high whistle.

When the drake moults during July and August dull plumage is necessary as he becomes flightless and cannot escape predators so easily. In an average year his full glory is regained by the beginning of the shooting season—1 September. Juveniles resemble the female and those from late broods ('flappers') should be avoided at the start of the shooting season, being left to provide better sport when stronger on the wing. Both sexes measure around 23 in but the

A female golden plover at her nest: one of our most exciting sporting quarry species.

93

drake's average weight is rather more than the duck's—2 lb 11 oz, compared with 2 lb 6 oz.

Courtship begins in autumn and pairing proper in November, though December is more usual. They are thought to pair for life and fly off to the breeding grounds early in the year.

The simple nest of leaves and grass lined with vegetation and down is found in a wide variety of freshwater and brackish habitats, usually on the ground in dense undergrowth. Some sites are several miles from water, in dry woodland or a tree hole as much as 30 ft high. Artificial sites such as wooden boxes and woven baskets are readily accepted.

Though some are laid earlier in mild weather, most clutches of ten to twelve (sometimes seven to sixteen) pale grey-green or olive-buff eggs are laid from March to May. In Britain two broods are common and these are incubated by the female alone for about twenty-eight days. The ducklings leave the nest soon after hatching, are usually tended by the mother only and led straight to water. Although fledged at about six and a half weeks, the ducklings may be tended for a further two weeks. Mortality is high: on average only two chicks fledge from a brood of eight to ten.

The mallard's diet is wide-ranging, much of it taken in shallow water where the bird can dabble, up-ending to reach the bottom and take aquatic vegetation. However, it never dives for food and is chiefly a night feeder. Staple foods of water plants are supplemented by animal foods ranging from insects to fish and earthworms. Good shooting opportunities are provided inland when mallard flight at dusk to feed on exposed potatoes softened by frost and on grain on stubbles. Very occasionally they also pull down standing corn to get at the ears.

Outside the breeding season mallard generally rest by day on or near water and flight to feed from late afternoon till soon after dusk, returning at dawn. Regular flights may be to inland marshes and rivers to feed on natural foods or to farmland, sometimes far from water, to feed on crops and weeds. However, flighting can be utterly unpredictable through a combination of factors such as local disturbance, weather, and tide. Sometimes they flight to the coast at dusk after resting on inland waters by day. As always, the sportsman must study local patterns to get good results.

After some decrease in the 1970s, our resident population has increased substantially. Breeding birds move little but there is some drifting southwards and towards the coast when hard weather sets in during the winter months. From September and October our breeding stock is joined by huge numbers of passage migrants and winter visitors from much colder places such as Iceland, Scandinavia, and eastern Europe.

The mallard swims well and lightly, as do all dabbling duck, and generally dives only when courting or wounded. Flushed birds rise powerfully and almost vertically from the water, and when a group is put up it almost always splits up. Birds continue to rise for some distance, with fast flight, though the wingbeats are slower than those of most duck. As with other wildfowl, the particular whistling of the wings aids identification in poor light.

Highly gregarious in winter, the mallard is always wary in regularly shot areas and truly wild birds must be treated with the same respect we have for more prized fowl such as wigeon. It is true that large numbers continue to be reared and released, though in recent years the emphasis has switched to improvement of habitat to increase stocks, and this does lead to some pretty tame shooting. In particular, some commercial shoots have reared large numbers of mallard on intensely fed inland waters and use these birds as a pathetic means to compensate for disappointing pheasant bags. This is not to say that reared duck cannot provide good sport, but the management must be excellent and the Guns well briefed to select only sporting targets. Otherwise we end up with duck being repeatedly forced off little waters to be massacred by inexperienced Guns who are only interested in getting their money's worth.

A splendid bird in the pot, the ubiquitous mallard remains the only species of duck many Guns will ever shoot but its quarry value is no less for that and its sporting potential is still widely underrated in Britain. Excavation of new waters under expert guidance such as that provided by the Game Conservancy is paving the way for further expansion of the sport.

## TEAL

After the mallard, the super-charged little teal is probably the duck most likely to be encountered by the all-round Shot. Widespread throughout Britain, it can pop up almost anywhere to surprise all but the most alert inland shooter as well as lovers of the saltmarsh.

Most of Scotland and Ireland have good breeding populations, but it is scarce in north-west Scotland. It breeds in most counties in north and east England, thinning out further south, but the south-west has very few pairs. In winter the distribution is very different with teal found widely inland and all around the coast.

British breeders tend to move south or south-west in autumn and a few even emigrate, especially in hard weather. Large numbers of passage migrants and winter visitors arrive chiefly in September and October from Iceland, Scandinavia, the Soviet Union, Poland, the Baltic, and the North Sea countries. They disperse rapidly, main concentrations being in south-east England, though large flocks do occur.

The teal does not breed easily in captivity and has never been the subject of widespread rearing and release. But it is relatively easy to encourage in the wild as in winter it takes to the smallest pond or even drainage dykes where there is sufficient cover. Unfortunately,

95

extensive land drainage and clearing of waters for fishing and other pursuits have destroyed much of its habitat.

In its breeding haunts the teal prefers rushy moorland, heath pools, bogs, peat mosses, and lochans. Lowland nest sites are less common but include lakes, rivers, streams, and freshwater and brackish marshes, providing there is sufficient vegetation. In winter, estuaries and mudflats are used extensively, though fresh water is preferred, including lakes, streams, reservoirs, sewage farms, and floods.

The nest is generally more closely associated with water than that of the mallard. A ground hollow in thick undergrowth is lined with dead leaves, other vegetation and down by the duck alone. The eight to twelve (occasionally fifteen) pale buff (sometimes tinged green) eggs are laid from late March to mid-May and the twenty-one-day incubation is by the female alone. The ducklings leave the nest soon after hatching, are tended mainly by the duck, and fly after about twenty-three days. There is just one brood and the devoted pairs probably remain together for life.

This tiny duck (average length 14 in for both sexes) is easy to identify. The male's average weight is 12 oz and the female's just 10 oz, but they provide one of the finest meals the wildfowler could ever hope to have. Apart from the small size, the metallic green and black speculum, and in flight the two white wing-bars, help to distinguish both sexes. Also note the drake's relatively dark head. The sound of the wings and rapid flight are also distinctive. Both sexes can be in eclipse from late July to October, but full plumage is mostly resumed by the end of September. As with other duck, eclipse and juvenile drakes resemble the female and can confuse inexperienced Guns during the first few weeks of the shooting season.

The drake utters a low, musical *crrick-crrick* call which is not at all duck-like, but the female has a short, high-pitched, bark-like quack. Flocks call continuously in flight, their *krit-krit* carrying a long way.

A dabbling duck, the teal feeds mainly on the surface in the shallows, but also up-ends in taking water weeds and their seeds, insects, and molluscs. More animal food, including worms, is taken in summer and in winter the emphasis is on aquatic seeds. Stubble-field grain is a great attraction in autumn and teal will flight several miles to reach it.

Most food is taken at night but day feeding is considerable in areas where there is little disturbance. Generally they spend the day resting on large waters or coastal marshes and fly out to small inland waters at dusk. They mostly follow regular routes and offer superbly testing sport as they flash low over the gloomy fields, curving, jinking, and weaving in unison, hugging contours and banking around woods—a great challenge for even the best of Shots. Lesser mortals rarely have the chance to discharge a second barrel before the birds are out of range. They tend to miss well behind and are no doubt confused by the sudden multiplicity of rocketing targets. However, a good Shot commonly takes several birds out of a bunch.

The teal is also excellent for walking-up. It holds fast in surprisingly scant cover until the Gun or his dog is right upon it. But its explosive reaction to danger is worth waiting for (having given rise to the popular Springing Teal stand in clay-pigeon shooting), the bird catapulting almost vertically into the air, thrusting swiftly away with rapid wingbeats, swerving and twisting to avoid death, as it needs to when pursued by a predator in its often well-wooded natural habitat.

Teal are highly gregarious and even large flocks bunch and twist as one, just like waders. And like snipe, they often suddenly drop down again into cover after being flushed. In low flight there is no regular formation but long-distance flights are much higher and often in v formation or lines.

In recent years the teal population has been in the ascendant, though Britain may well harbour about half the midwinter European population, so we must monitor the species' welfare very carefully. Over-shooting is unlikely ever to be a major threat as the bird is too quick for most Guns. The chief problem remains habitat abuse and destruction.

## WIGEON

The wigeon is probably the wildfowler's favourite duck. Although in recent years it has increasingly visited floods, lakes, and reservoirs near the coast, it remains chiefly a bird of the saltmarsh and muddy shorelines, so few inland Guns will get the chance to shoot it.

Only a few hundred pairs of wigeon nest in Britain—chiefly along the upland spine of England and Scotland from Yorkshire and Cumbria to the Pentland Firth—but in some recent years the UK has been host to well over 200,000 winter visitors. The British Isles attracts about half the total wigeon population of North-West Europe because of our generally mild winters and abundance of suitable coastal habitat. We receive most of the Icelandic birds plus others from Russia, Siberia, and Scandinavia. They arrive from the end of September and keep coming into the first half of November. Birds drift south as the cold intensifies, so the best shooting in the north is early in the season. Some of the major concentrations are in south-west and north-east Scotland and east and south-east England, where flocks of tens of thousands gather on estuaries. South-coast Guns usually enjoy fair sport but the farther west the more they are dependent on cold weather.

The male wigeon is the only British duck to have a white patch on the forewing and, seen from below, its dark head contrasts well with the white underparts. The female is slightly slimmer than the female mallard and both sexes have a distinctive rounded head, pointed tail, and green speculum. Compared with those of other duck, the wings are long and narrow and in flight come down well below the body. Birds may be in eclipse as late as November and in this the male looks like a dark female. The female has two colour types—one mainly brown, the other grey—possibly linked with age. The juvenile looks like a dull female right through to February, when males acquire their full splendour. The average adult's length is 18 in and weight 1 lb 15 oz for the male and 1 lb 11 oz the female.

The wigeon's call is very distinctive and one of the most evocative sounds of the saltmarsh. The drake's high-pitched, whistling *whee-oo* maintains flight contact between individuals and often gives the waiting wildfowler plenty of warning of a flock's approach. The female's low, growling purr is often heard as birds rest on inshore waters by day waiting for the tide to recede or for the cloak of night.

Only one clutch of seven to eight (sometimes six to ten) creamy-buff eggs is laid from late April to May and incubated by the female alone for twenty-two to twenty-five days. The ducklings leave the nest soon after hatching, are tended by the female alone, and attain independence on fledging at about six weeks.

A dabbling duck, the wigeon feeds mainly on eelgrass, the marine plant *Zostera*, which it grazes at low tide or, if the tide is still in, by pulling it up by the roots while paddling in the shallows, or by up-ending, at which it is rather clumsy. Unfortunately, in some major haunts *Zostera* has declined through disease, pollution, and the spread of *Spartina* grass. A greatly increased brent goose population may also be significant as this bird competes for the *Zostera*.

Where *Zostera* is unavailable, wigeon visit inland marshes and floods to feed mainly on grass, but also some seeds, grain, and animal foods. Early immigrants are mostly naïve, immature birds which openly feed by day and are relatively easy to approach, but the nocturnal habit soon takes over in disturbed areas. Mature birds also feed by day in undisturbed areas. They are frequently shot under the moon, when they are more likely to move about in small flocks. For shooting success, local study of flighting patterns is essential.

Wigeon are highly gregarious in winter but the large flocks which form in estuaries and harbours and on mudflats and sandbars remain shy and wary. At the slightest hint of danger they swim smoothly away or rise swiftly together, moving off rapidly with powerful flight, evasively where necessary. However, they respond well to most duck decoys and usually provide good sporting opportunities, gliding in on arched wings. Wounded birds dive well to avoid capture by retrievers and easily get the better of an inexperienced dog, especially in a strong current.

Sometimes strong-flavoured, wigeon may need skilful and imaginative cooking, but the man who puts one in the pot is always a competent and satisfied hunter.

## PINTAIL

By far the fastest British quarry duck, the pintail is a great favourite among wildfowlers. It is also our rarest breeding dabbling duck, Britain holding a mere 50 or so pairs, yet it is possibly the most abundant duck in the world. Every year, from September, Britain hosts some 25,000 to 30,000 winter visitors and passage migrants from Iceland, Scandinavia, and northern Russia.

As a breeding species, the pintail appears to have colonized Britain in the nineteenth century and sites remain curiously scattered. The chief centres are the North Kent Marshes and the Fens. The species is semi-colonial and the nest hollow is frequently more exposed than those of other duck, being in short grass on open ground, though they do occur in longer vegetation, usually close to water.

The single brood of seven to nine (occasionally six to twelve) mainly olive-green eggs is laid from mid-April in the south to mid-June in the north and incubated by the female alone for twenty-one to twenty-three days. The ducklings leave the nest soon after hatching and fly after about four weeks, though the female tends them for a further three weeks.

In winter the pintail favours mainly shallow coasts and sheltered estuaries and generally only those waters and floods near the sea will be visited as the species is almost entirely maritime in this season. Particularly large concentrations occur on the Dee, Ouse Washes, Ribble, Medway, and Martin Mere.

The handsome drake's two sharply pointed central tail feathers give rise to the bird's name and provide the best means of identification. The female's tail is also long and pointed, though less so than the male's. She is slighter and greyer than the female mallard, with a slender bill and no distinct speculum, and in flight has a noticeable pale trailing edge to the wing. The drake's chocolate hood contrasts well with his white breast and belly. Both sexes are relatively long-necked and graceful.

In eclipse the male resembles the female, but with darker upper-parts, full plumage usually being regained by the end of October. Juveniles look like darker, more uniformly coloured females, the young drake being greyer and without noticeably long central tail feathers. Average length of the male is 26 in, with a tail to 8 in, and the female 22 in, both weighing about 1½ lb.

Although mostly a quiet species, especially by day, a feeding flock sometimes produces a low chattering. The drake has a low double whistle, a low *kah* or *kruck* and a nasal, wheezing *gzeee*. Much less strident than that of the mallard, the female's subdued quack carries a long distance and is often given as an alarm signal. This wary duck often associates with wigeon and other fowl and is usually the first to take wing at any sign of danger.

Flight is direct, with very fast wingbeats, which make a strange swishing sound unlike that of any other British duck. Flocks often fly in v formation or long lines.

In winter the pintail generally rests offshore, in large flocks or small parties, and flights inshore to feed only after dark, returning before dawn. Even where disturbance is minimal it is mainly a nocturnal feeder. This surface-feeder up-ends to take mainly water plants, molluscs, some freshwater insects, and worms, mostly from bottom mud and in shallow water. Stubbles and grass fields are also visited and roots may be unearthed.

The pintail makes a delicious meal.

## SHOVELER

The very active shoveler, which gets its name from its proportionately large, 3 in bill, is not shot in anything like the numbers of mallard, wigeon, and teal, or even pintail, but it provides fair sport.

Always wary, with man about it keeps well out on water, swimming apparently front-heavy with the bill tilted down. It dives more than other surface feeders, especially when alarmed.

It rises quite easily from the water, with a distinctive drumming rattle of wings, and once underway the wings whistle characteristically. Flight is powerful and fast, with rapid wingbeats, though less speedy than apparent, and certainly slower than that of the mallard. It resembles the wigeon's but twists and turns more.

Less gregarious than the other dabbling duck, the shoveler feeds mostly in small parties but may gather in large numbers at favoured roosts. It uses the comb-like structure on the sides of the beak to sieve out tiny plants and animals from thin mud and water while it paddles quickly through the shallows, mostly with the head and neck submerged, the spoon-like bill held forward, sweeping from side to side. The wide variety of foods—animal and vegetable in approximately equal amounts—includes freshwater crustaceans, molluscs and insects, and the buds, leaves, and seeds of water plants.

In Britain the shoveler enjoyed major increase and range expansion over the first half of this century, possibly due to temporary climatic amelioration, but since the last war greatly increased land drainage has severely reduced its already very restricted marsh habitat. Its spatulate bill is suitable only for shallow, eutrophic waters, so throughout the year the shoveler is usually found only on brackish and fresh water. Breeding birds need stillwaters with shallow edges and plenty of weeds, marshland pools, drainage dykes, and well-watered grazing marshes. In winter, estuaries on low-lying coasts and floods, chiefly on meadows bordering lakes, are important.

The British breeding range is restricted by the very specialist feeding and habitat requirements, suitable shallow, muddy waters being found only in the lowlands. Nowhere do they breed above 400 ft. Thus the greatest concentrations of the 1,000 or so pairs are in the south-east between the Thames Estuary and the Wash. Elsewhere groups are more isolated. Fortunately, our winter distribution is much wider, though very local.

Most British and Irish birds migrate south to winter in France and beyond but about 9,000 come here as passage migrants and winter visitors from Iceland, Scandinavia, Russia, and Northern and Eastern Europe, arriving between September and November.

The shoveler's best field mark is its big spatulate bill—narrow at the base and longer than the head, being especially noticeable in flight. The drake's chestnut belly contrasts well with the white chest and dark head and the sky-blue forewing is prominent. The female's blue is much duller, but she may be distinguished from the female mallard by her bill, smaller size, heavier build, shorter neck, and different carriage. Juveniles look like dull females. In eclipse the drake resembles the female, even assuming her bill colour, but is more uniformly coloured, with a darker back and more colour on the wing. His eclipse is long, starting in May or June, and he may not regain his full colour until January, though mid-July to the end of September is more usual.

Flying birds appear to have their wings set well back on their bodies, but this is partly due to the disproportionate effect of the great bill. For both sexes average length is 20 in and weight 1 lb 6 oz. They are very quiet outside the breeding season but the male has a throaty *took-took* and a loud, nasal *paay*, and the female's loud, croaking double quack, sometimes in decrescendo, is mallard-like.

The ground nest is mostly well hidden in tall vegetation, though sometimes in open situations such as in bogs and on reservoir banks. The single clutch of eight to twelve (sometimes seven to fourteen) buff or green eggs is laid from late April to May and incubated by the female alone for some twenty-three to twenty-four days. The ugly (chiefly because of their bills) ducklings leave the nest soon after hatching, fly after some six weeks, and are often tended by the female for a further week.

Though the least palatable of the generally appetizing dabbling duck, the shoveler is variable in flavour and is said to make a good meal when the animal content in its diet is low.

### GADWALL

The least known of our hunted dabbling duck, the gadwall numbers only some 3,000 in the British Isles in winter. But it remains on our quarry list because it is very common elsewhere and its population and range are increasing. It is also very sporting and among the most delicious of fowl.

First recorded British breeding was from a wing-clipped pair turned

down in the Brecks in about 1850. Since then, with the aid of an increasing number of winter visitors, feral flocks, and a steadily increasing world population, the British breeding population has grown to some 500 pairs. The greatest concentration is in East Anglia, with the other main outposts along the Essex and Kent coasts, in parts of Surrey, the south-west, Yorkshire, Northern Ireland and south-east Scotland.

The winter distribution is much wider, though local. English breeders are mostly resident, while Scottish birds move south to England and Ireland. Winter visitors arrive from Iceland, the Baltic, the North Sea countries, and the Continent from mid-August, peaking in October and tailing off in November, but after resting on coasts and estuaries soon move to quiet inland waters.

Shallow, lowland freshwaters with thick vegetation are preferred, but some reservoirs, slow-moving streams, lakes, marshes, meres, and floods are also used. A greater variety of waters is used in winter.

The gadwall concentrates on vegetable food such as leaves, roots, and the seeds and buds of water plants, much taken by immersing the head, but it rarely up-ends. Animal food includes worms and snails. Farmland is sometimes grazed and the stubbles visited in autumn. Where undisturbed it feeds chiefly by day but it is a wary and restless bird that spends much time flying between roost and feeding ground. It loves to creep among dense vegetation but mixes well with other duck and is usually one of the first species to respond to danger. It is seldom seen in large numbers.

Despite faster wingbeats, the gadwall's wigeon-like flight is slower than the mallard's and the whistling of its wings is lower-pitched. Both sexes appear grey-brown at a distance but both are distinguished by the white wing-bar—unique among British duck. Also distinctive are the male's largely white underparts, contrasting with the dark head and neck, and his black undertail coverts. The juvenile is distinguished from the female by darker upperparts and streaks and spots below. In eclipse the drake loses the crescent markings on the breast and his bill assumes the colour of the duck's. The return to full plumage may be as early as June but is rarely complete by mid-October. The wings are more pointed than the mallard's and the average body length 20 in.

The female's soft quack sounds more excited than that of the mallard, being higher-pitched, uttered more frequently, and dropping off at the end of a series. The drake's calls include a soft whistle and a single croaking note.

## TUFTED DUCK

By far the most widespread of Britain's three species of diving duck still on the quarry list, the tufted has gained greatly through man's creation of new waters, particularly lakes created by gravel extraction and reservoirs for town water supply. It prefers large inland stillwaters, especially those fringed with dense, aquatic vegetation, but quiet rivers and city lakes and ponds are also used. Vegetation is less important in winter, when bare reservoirs, and to a lesser extent estuaries and calmer coastal waters, are also frequented. Saltwater and brackish haunts are mostly avoided, except during migration and severe frost.

The first recorded British breeding was in 1849, but now the UK has some 7,000 pairs, most generally keeping to waters of at least a couple of acres, and below about 1,300 ft. Summer distribution is very widespread, but sparse among the hills of the north and west. In winter the greatest concentrations are on the reservoirs of the south and east of England.

One of the easiest duck to identify, the black-and-white male has a long, neat crest drooping from the hind crown. The rich dark-brown female has a much shorter crest, though still appears to have an angular head. Both sexes have a white bar right across the wing. The juvenile looks like a dull female and in eclipse the drake resembles a dark female. He rarely regains full handsome plumage before December. Average length is 17 in and average weight 1 lb 9 oz.

In winter this is a quiet species, though the female utters a harsh, crow-like *karr-karr* on rising in alarm and sometimes a gentler, rolling note. The male has a soft courtship whistle.

Nest-sites must be near limestone or other non-acidic formations. Most are on dry ground in thick vegetation very close to water, but sometimes over water on reed platforms or old coot nests. Communal breeding is not unusual on islands. They probably pair for life.

The single brood of five to twelve (up to eighteen recorded) pale grey-green eggs is mostly laid rather late—from mid-May, though sometimes from mid-April. Incubation, by the female alone, is for about twenty-four days and broods are seldom seen before the end of June. Ducklings swim and dive within a few hours, are tended by the female alone, and fledge at about six weeks.

Most food taken is animal—insects, molluscs, crustaceans, frog-spawn, tadpoles, frogs, small fish, etc. Leaves and seeds of water plants are taken in varying proportions, according to local abundance.

Most feeding takes place in waters 10-45 ft deep, considerably deeper than those favoured by the pochard. Birds may feed and roost at the same site, feeding by day where undisturbed, mostly morning and evening. However, they are chiefly night feeders.

Some 50,000 passage migrants and winter visitors swell the resident British population, which drifts south in winter but does not usually emigrate. Birds from Iceland, Scandinavia, North-West Europe, and Russia arrive from mid-September to the end of November. They peak in October before many have continued to Ireland. In severe frost many carry on to France.

A gregarious bird, the 'tuftie' is usually found in parties of a few dozen, and in winter may form huge rafts in association with pochards and coots. Away from the park or urban environment it is a wary bird and rarely visits land outside the breeding season. On inland waters during the day it usually keeps well out from the shore, often preening and sleeping near the centre of a lake.

One of our best divers, the tufted commonly submerges for over a minute. Pursued birds always prefer to dive or swim away rather than fly and it is not unusual for several hundred to dive simultaneously at the sound of a shot.

It takes off more easily than the pochard, though strikes the surface noisily with the feet, in the manner of coots. Flight is direct, smooth and fast, with rapid wingbeats, and the wings make a distinctive rustling.

## POCHARD

Faster than the mallard, the pochard provides good sport. But this duck is a reluctant flier, preferring to swim farther out at the approach of danger. In fact, most of its time is spent on water, where it dives frequently and well. With the legs set well back on the body, it is front-heavy and clumsy on land.

When it does take off it is slow to get going, having to patter across the water like other diving duck, usually rising into the wind with rapid wingbeats. Flight is fast and direct, usually in compact formations, but on longer flights they often form long, irregular lines or ragged spearheads. Landing is often very clumsy.

The pochard has enjoyed a slow but steady increase, colonizing much of Britain, Scandinavia, and Europe since the mid-nineteenth century. However, the total British Isles' breeding population is still probably under 400 pairs and there has been a marked decline in Scotland. It breeds very locally, perhaps half being found in coastal counties from Kent to Lincolnshire, with Hampshire and Greater London next in importance.

However, in winter it is very widely distributed, with some 50,000 passage migrants and winter visitors arriving in Britain from northern Europe, Iceland, and the USSR between September and November. They soon disperse to inland waters and resident birds move away from their nesting areas. Small parties are often seen on town-park lakes but most big assemblies are on large waters such as reservoirs, lakes and gravel pits. The greatest concentrations are in central and southern England as well as the Scottish lowlands. Some areas have flocks of over 1,000, including some of the London reservoirs. Although freshwater is always preferred, wintering birds are found on estuaries and sheltered brackish waters. But in spite of this, it is never a truly maritime species.

For breeding it requires thick emergent and waterside vegetation around large stillwaters, preferring overgrown islands, though slow-moving streams, marshes, and smaller waters are used in areas of high density. Gravel pits and reservoirs are rarely used as they do not usually have sufficient aquatic vegetation. Nests are usually below 1,000 ft.

The duck uses down to line her nest on a substantial base of aquatic vegetation over water, in reedbeds, or thick growth near open water. The single clutch of six to eleven (up to eighteen recorded) grey-green eggs is laid from mid-April to early May and incubated by the female alone for twenty-four to twenty-six days. Within a few hours of hatching the ducklings swim well. Tended by the female alone, they fly at seven to eight weeks.

Mostly vegetable food—roots, buds, and leaves of aquatic plants— is taken from water 3-8 ft deep. According to availability, small water animals, fish, and tadpoles are also eaten. Occasionally the pochard up-ends like surface-feeding duck. It feeds by day where undisturbed but is most active early and late in the night and there are often strong dusk and dawn flights to better food waters.

The drake is easily identified by his chestnut-red head and neck, very pale grey upperparts and flanks. In flight the absence of a white bar on their grey wings distinguishes both sexes from the tufted duck. In eclipse the male looks like a greyer-backed female and it is sometimes well into the shooting season before full plumage is regained. Juveniles closely resemble the female. The average length of both sexes is 18 in and average weight 1 lb 13 oz.

A quiet species outside courtship, the male has a low, soft whistle and a nasal call and the female a low, harsh, rasping croak—*kurr* or *karr*.

## GOLDENEYE

Unlike our two other species of diving quarry duck, the goldeneye is mainly a coastal bird in winter and a great favourite with wildfowlers. Although less gregarious than most duck, flocks of 1,000 or more are seen regularly at sites such as the Firth of Forth. It rarely mixes with other duck and on a shared water generally forms an exclusive goldeneye group.

Only about forty pairs breed in Britain, through lack of suitable nest-sites, but in Inverness-shire at least, nestboxes have aided colonization this century. Most natural sites are in deep tree hollows, though rabbit burrows or cavities under rocks or logs are sometimes used. Most nests are near freshwater.

The single clutch of six to eleven (up to fifteen recorded) blue-green eggs is laid in mid-April on wood chips, feathers, and down provided by the female, which incubates alone for some thirty days. The young tumble to the ground and are taken to the nearest water by the female just one day after hatching. They

105

fledge at about eight to nine weeks but are quite independent at seven weeks.

About 15,000 goldeneye have wintered in or passed through Britain in recent years. These immigrants, mostly from Scandinavia, arrive from mid-September to November. They favour Scotland but there are many good English locations and the thin but wide distribution includes much of Wales and Ireland. Most concentrate on the less icy estuaries, coasts, and sheltered bays, especially in midwinter. Small groups also use suitable freshwaters, unless frost is severe.

The golden eye, which gives the bird its name, is not a good field mark but the white, circular patch between the drake's bill and eye is noticeable at considerable distances. The curious, triangular head identifies both sexes, even at long range, and in flight the squat shape, white wing-bar and short neck are noticeable. The male is mainly black-and-white, with a green sheen on the head, and the female is grey with a brown head and white collar. In eclipse the male resembles the female but retains some dark-green head feathers. Full plumage is regained between the end of October and Christmas. Juveniles are like dull females and lack the white shoulders. The average adult length is 18 in and weight 1 lb 13 oz.

Generally a very quiet species, the male makes a harsh, wheezing *zeee-zeee* and the female a growling *kurr*, a rapid *kah-kah-kah* and a screech.

Feeding concentrates on animal food in water up to 13 ft deep, always near the shore when on the coast. Food includes molluscs, small fish, crustaceans, aquatic vegetation, insects, tadpoles, leeches, and shrimps, much of it taken by probing with the strong bill on water beds. The goldeneye is chiefly a day feeder but in winter, when it may roost far from feeding grounds, and in disturbed areas, it may flight at night to feed on fresh lakes or quiet, brackish waters.

On approach of danger the goldeneye usually dives and reappears farther away, and even when not pressed seems to prefer travelling underwater. Like other diving duck, it is clumsy on land, which is rarely visited. However, it is a restless bird and spends much time on the wing. Unlike other diving duck, it rises directly into the air rather than pattering across the water, though it may strike the surface a few times with its feet when there is little or no wind. Flight is strong and fast, the rapid wingbeats producing a whistling rattle.

## CANADA GOOSE

Unlike the other three species of goose on the British quarry list, the Canada is not truly migratory in this country and provides substantial sport for inland shooters in central and southern England. Introduced from North America in 1678, to grace the lakes of wealthy landowners, the species soon established feral flocks and has enjoyed sustained population growth, numbering well over 45,000 in Britain today. It is the most numerous goose in the world.

Since its naturalization in Britain, the bird's habits have changed considerably and increasingly it offers good shooting. Where they do not flight at all, sport can be poor but they soon become wary after a few shots and considerable fieldcraft may be necessary to get within range.

British Canadas do not generally flight very high and they appear deceptively slow and heavy. In fact they are fast and direct—probably even faster than grey geese. On longer journeys the familiar v formation may be adopted.

There is little seasonal variation in British distribution, but in winter some birds leave inland haunts to feed on saltmarshes and in estuaries, some flights being quite regular, though erratic as to precise line. However, a moult migration to Scotland started in Yorkshire in the 1950s and the habit is spreading to birds farther and farther south. About 50 per cent immatures (one to two years old) and 50 per cent adult non-breeders, these birds mostly spend June to August on the Beauly Firth in Inverness-shire.

The Canada is widespread over most of lowland England but sparsely distributed in Wales and Scotland. There is a good Northern Ireland population centred on Strangford Lough and in 1987 the species was added to the Ulster shooting list. Several English locations have concentrations of over 1,000 birds.

The species' natural North American habitat is marsh and lake in wooded country, but in Britain the unnatural emphasis is on park lakes. As the population has grown birds have also taken to breeding on town lakes, flooded gravel pits, reservoirs with marginal vegetation, slow-moving rivers, and marshes. Small ponds, flooded meadows, and sheltered harbours are used less frequently.

This goose is very easy to identify, the best field marks being the white cheek-patch contrasting with the black head and neck, the white undertail-coverts, and the dark grey-brown upperparts. The sexes are alike but there is considerable variation in the size and colour of individuals. In its first winter the juvenile is virtually indistinguishable from the adult in the field, but is somewhat duller, with pale edges to the wing-coverts and a darker chin strap.

Our two other 'black' geese—the barnacle and brent—are much smaller and black and grey rather than brown on the body. The Canada's black head and neck readily distinguish it from the 'grey' geese. The average length is 36-40 in and average weight 10 lb 12 oz for the male and 9 lb 11 oz for the female. The species' main call is most distinctive—a far-carrying *aa-honk* in flight.

Canadas are colonial nesters on large waters, where islands are preferred. The single clutch of five or six (two to eleven recorded) dirty-white eggs is laid between early April and the end of May in a ground nest lined with grass, dead leaves, and down. The female incubates alone for twenty-eight to thirty days while the male mounts

guard nearby. The goslings leave the nest soon after hatching, are tended by both parents, fledge at about nine weeks, and remain with the parents throughout the winter.

Almost all food taken is vegetable, chiefly grass through much of the year, but in autumn there is concentration on stubbles in some areas. Crops may be trampled and Canadas do walk into standing cereals to strip seeds, but few areas have populations large enough to cause substantial losses. However, the continued population growth is of concern to farmers, especially where cereals are adjacent to breeding or moulting waters. Grass losses too can be substantial, especially in spring. The diet also includes some water plants, sedges, and clover as well as insects in summer.

Feeding is mostly by day, birds often walking from the roost to nearby feeding grounds if there are no obstacles. Most feeding journeys are short, though a few cover over twenty miles, sometimes providing good shooting along the way, though flighting times may be unpredictable.

Agricultural pest it may be, but the Canada goose provides an excellent meal and as its numbers grow more and more people will value the opportunity to engage an increasingly sporting quarry.

Introduced from North America in 1678, the Canada goose has thrived in Britain and increasingly offers good sport.

### GREYLAG GOOSE

Although the ancestor of many farmyard geese, the greylag remains one of Britain's most exciting quarry species. We have a small breeding population but the greatest sporting interest is in the entire Icelandic population, which winters in the British Isles along with a few others from Scandinavia and North-West Europe. In recent years well over 100,000 birds have arrived in Scotland (150,000 in 1987/8), mostly in late October and November. Many go straight to northern England or Ireland, according to the year's weather and harvest.

In Britain truly native birds are found only in the Outer Hebrides and parts of the nearby Scottish mainland, totalling under 200 wild pairs. Sadly, much of their habitat is now threatened by afforestation. But there is a growing feral population of at least 600 pairs derived from introduced stock, notably on the Scottish Solway, in the southern Lake District, Norfolk, County Down, the Midlands, and Kent. Many of these flocks cause increasing agricultural damage.

The greylag constantly changes its winter distribution in response to weather and available food, but generally the main concentrations are on the Scottish lochs and firths, in agricultural areas in central and eastern Scotland, and parts of northern England and eastern Ireland. Parts of the Midlands and eastern England have much smaller, more variable numbers of visitors. Dispersal is much greater in wet weather with an abundance of inland floods.

Scottish breeding sites include heather moorland with scattered lochs, the threatened herb-rich grassland of the Machair of the Outer

Hebrides, and small coastal islands. Feral birds are much less shy and use a wide variety of waters. In winter many large fresh, brackish, and salt waters are used, especially those near feeding areas.

The nest is always well hidden in reeds or thick vegetation near water. The single clutch of four to six (sometimes three to nine) white eggs is laid between late March and May and incubated by the female alone for twenty-seven to twenty-eight days while the male keeps watch nearby. The goslings leave the nest within a few hours of hatching, are tended by both parents, fly after about eight weeks, and remain in family parties until well into the winter. Families often join up to form large gatherings.

Grey geese are not easy to identify, especially as they show considerable individual plumage variation. The greylag's general colouring is grey-brown and note that at rest its folded wings do not reach beyond the end of the tail. The back is barred, the large bill orange with an ivory nail, the head heavy, the neck thick, the legs and feet pink, and the rump pale grey. In flight watch for the very pale grey forewing (absent in our other geese) contrasting with the darker saddle and primaries. Generally larger and paler than the other grey geese, the sexes are alike. The juvenile has less definite transverse lines on the back, less continuous pale edge to the folded wing, paler bill and legs, and a general lack of flecks. The average adult length is 30-35 in and weight 8 lb 6 oz for the male and 7 lb the female.

At great height calls are more important in identifying grey geese. The most familiar of the greylag's wide range of calls is the deep, throaty *aahng-ung-ung* of two to four syllables. The clamour of a distant flock has been likened to a pack of hounds in full cry and it is very exciting as the wildfowler tries to pinpoint the far-carrying calls of an approaching skein.

The species has been very successful in exploiting changing agricultural practices, but this has often brought it into conflict with man. Scottish farmers have long welcomed sportsmen to control the geese. For many years such sport was mostly free, but sadly, in recent years, the spread of commercialism has led to considerable over-shooting. In some cases excessive bags have been made and in others unscrupulous farmers have let shooting where hardly any geese visit.

The greylag has benefited enormously through the northward spread of barley this century. Early in the shooting season 70 per cent of birds feed on barley and oat stubble and the remainder on grass. A little grain is also taken from standing stalks around field edges.

As the stubbles are ploughed-in, the geese turn more to grass and root crops and occasionally dig up unharvested potatoes, though most potatoes taken are those left on the surface after harvest and softened by frost. By November most potatoes are gone as most fields are then planted with winter wheat.

110

Grazing of winter wheat can be locally serious in wet conditions, when the birds puddle the fields excessively, and in early spring, when the geese are still here, loss of grass is a worry for the farmer as early growth is particularly valuable in improving milk yields and the condition of stock. Also in Scotland swedes are taken regularly, and in severe weather rape, kale, and brassicae.

Where undisturbed, inland feeding is mostly by day, the geese flighting to the feeding grounds at dawn or soon after and returning to roost at dusk. However, in tidal areas most feeding is nocturnal, beginning about two hours before sunset and ending soon after sunrise. In addition, when the moon is bright, geese will flight to feed and remain on the fields while it is up, after which the birds may flight to the coast to take grit in the form of sand to aid digestion. The sportsman must always study local patterns to stand a chance of a shot.

Though mostly very wary, greylags can be easy to approach when feeding in small fields close to cover and they will even graze near livestock and eat roots put out for sheep. Immature birds are particularly naïve and have occasionally formed the bulk of unjustifi-ably large bags, especially over decoys.

Roosts are generally in inaccessible places with a good all-round view, but greylags are less cautious than other geese and often use small lakes and floods, where they usually sleep on the margins rather than the water, as well as estuaries, large lakes, and sandbanks.

Flight is direct, powerful, and deceptively fast—so much so that most novice goose shooters miss way behind with their first shots.

In flighting geese, light is probably the most important considera-tion for the wildfowler, but weather, wind, and tide also help to determine the line of flight, the height at which birds come in, and to a lesser extent, their time of arrival. Geese are more regular in fine weather but the fowler prefers stormy conditions as then the birds fly lower and in smaller parties, so that the flight lasts longer.

Strong wind can alter the line of approach by as much as two miles or so. Geese prefer to drift way off line before turning to drive into a strong wind towards their target. When they come in high and out of range in still conditions their great size can make them look deceptively low and then irresponsible or inexperienced Guns may shoot at them through ignorance or hope to bring off a fluke shot, but generally succeed only in wounding a few. Good tuition and experience of range judging are particularly important in goose shooting.

Snow and fog make geese fly low but then they are very unpredictable. Tide too affects their routine. For example, an early flood may wash them off their feet before dawn so that they start to flight some miles wide of their roost.

Evening flight is generally much shorter as the birds assemble in large flocks and keep together more, regardless of conditions. Only on

Greylag geese are among Britain's most prized quarry species, and their population continues to rise as they successfully exploit modern agriculture.

moonless evenings are the geese punctual to dusk. Moonlight makes the birds uneasy and they will not often flight until it is gone. A flight will be postponed when there is snow on the ground, and bright starlight may also upset the routine.

On the short days of midwinter, geese generally flight earlier in the morning and return later in the evening to maximize feeding time and get sufficient energy. Departure and arrival times will also vary with the distance between roost and feeding gound. Thus the consistently successful goose shooter must be a patient and good observer.

With its population thriving, the greylag is providing excellent sport for more and more people. However, excessive commercialism is leading to abuse of the sanctity of roosts and without generally undisturbed resting places geese cannot exploit new feeding grounds. Most wildfowlers have long valued the greylag as a worthy quarry and an excellent meal but there is a new breed of cowboy who always wants to bag his money's worth. Every sportsman must guard against such action and point the miscreants in the right direction.

### PINKFOOTED GOOSE

Much of what has been said about the behaviour and shooting of the greylag also applies to the pinkfoot, the smallest of British grey geese. In most years it is at least as numerous as the greylag but none breed in Britain. (In the winter of 1987/88 a record 160,000 visited Britain.) The species' breeding range is confined to the east coast of Greenland, Iceland, and Spitzbergen, and as the entire Greenland/ Iceland population winters in the British Isles we have a great international responsibility for the species.

The chief centre is in eastern Scotland, but pinkfeet also visit northern England, the Wash, and Ireland, the Solway being particularly important in spring. Numbers and range have grown with the acreage of cereals this century, though this is very much at the mercy of the weather. However, a more efficiently gathered Scottish grain harvest in the early 1970s meant less food available for pinkfeet and the birds were forced to forage farther south. They then found the crops (especially carrots) of the Lancashire Mosses and since then tens of thousands have continued to visit the area, where they cause considerable economic loss. In Britain most birds winter on estuaries, coasts, and lakes, and to a lesser extent moors, within range of feeding grounds.

At most distances the pinkfoot's best field marks are the dark head and neck contrasting with the light body. It is the greyest of our grey geese and at rest, unlike those of the heavier greylag, the folded wings reach beyond the end of the tail. No other goose has pink on the bill *and* pink legs. The sexes are alike. Juveniles are darker and browner above, quite mottled below and generally duller and less rounded than the adults in early winter. Their wing-coverts have less

distinct pale edges than those of the adults. The average adult length is 24-30 in and weight 6 lb 2 oz the male and 5 lb 9 oz the female.

More noisy than most wildfowl, the pinkfoot has some distinctive shrill calls—*wink-wink* or *wink-wink-wink ung-ung* or *ung-unk.*

On the breeding grounds pinkfeet take insects, leaves and flowers of plants around the nest, roots, shoots, grass, berries, and seeds of bog plants. But in winter the large British population is virtually dependent on agriculture, though some wild shoots and roots are taken. Early in the season stubble grain is the main attraction, but the pinkfoot is more fussy than the greylag and barley is preferred. Such grain is more easily collected than wild seeds, more nutritious, and more easily digested. When the stubbles are ploughed-in, pinkfeet turn to ley or pasture grass and potatoes.

Although only the tops of roots, such as carrots, and brassicae are eaten, the crops are still unsaleable and financial loss may be considerable. Damage to winter corn may be great too, especially in floods on heavy soils. But the main winter target is grass, especially where heavily fertilized. Grassland grazing is mostly insignificant, except at high density in spring when there is competition with livestock.

Pinkfeet feed mostly by day unless greatly disturbed, flying in at dawn or soon after and returning to roost at dusk. But when the moon is bright they may feed at night, flighting to the shore at dawn to take sand to aid digestion. This is the species of goose most frequently shot under the moon, though few fowlers are hardy or skilled enough to go moonflighting.

Most pinkfeet arrive in early October and concentrate on inland or upland farms before settling down in lowland marshes in November. Some fly straight to their eventual wintering areas farther south.

This highly gregarious bird often assembles in flocks of several thousands which break up as winter progresses, partially reuniting again in spring, chiefly in southern and east-central Scotland. Loch roosts can contain huge flocks, but larger sites, especially estuarine mudflats, are preferred when near feeding grounds. Pinkfeet are mostly very wary, so roosts are inevitably inaccessible places, but at a freshwater roost they usually sleep on the margins rather than the water. From day-feeding grounds they sometimes return to a nearby roost at midday to drink and bathe, but when feeding far from the main roost they may establish a subsidiary roost in a fairly safe spot near the feeding ground and take a midday break there.

Flight is fast and direct and flighting habits are generally similar to those of the greylag. In particular, they will not visit feeding grounds until the light is sufficient to see predators by and will leave again when the light level drops. The safer the area the more likely they are to feed at night and moonlight feeding is more common when daylight is short.

## WHITEFRONTED GOOSE

The whitefront does not breed in Britain but every winter these islands are host to two distinct races which come from opposite directions to enjoy our mild climate. At present, whitefronts of any race may be shot in England and Wales only. There has been licensed shooting of Greenland whitefronts in areas of great concentration on Islay, where farmers have suffered economic loss, but calls for reinstatement to the Scottish quarry list are unwise in view of the species' overall vulnerability.

The European race breeds widely in arctic Russia and Siberia and each year some 8,000 arrive in southern and eastern England and Wales between October and January, the main resorts being Slimbridge (Gloucestershire), the Swale (Kent), the Avon (Hampshire), the North Kent Marshes, and Dryslwyn (Dyfed). It appears to be in the ascendant, whereas the Greenland race has had a bad time through poor breeding years and the destruction of its habitat. The latter breeds only in western Greenland and winters almost entirely in Ireland, western Scotland, and western Wales, only a few visiting England (mainly north-west). Some 6-7,000 visit Scotland (notably Islay and the western isles, Kintyre at Campbeltown and opposite Gigha, and Loch Ken), and Wales (mostly Tregaron and Anglesey) while some 8,000 go to Ireland. Yet it is still the most common *grey* goose in winter in the western British Isles.

Of the grey geese the whitefront is the easiest to recognize, with the white feathers around the base of the upper mandible and the black-barred underparts (very variable) clearly visible at rest and in flight within shooting range. The European race is paler and slightly smaller than the Greenland and the European's pink bill is shorter than the yellow-orange bill of the Greenland, the European usually having more white at the base of the bill.

The sexes are alike. Juveniles lack the barring underneath and the white at the base of the bill, the latter appearing late in the winter and the black belly markings in the following summer. The average length is 26-30 in and average weight 5 lb 10 oz for the male and 5 lb 1 oz the female.

Known as the 'laughing goose', the whitefront has a high-pitched, gabbling *kow-yow* or *kow-lyow* call which is louder and more musical than the pinkfoot's. There is also a *gar-wa-wa* call.

Much less dependent on farming than the other grey geese, the whitefront feeds mostly on vegetable matter. In Britain the chief winter food is grass, flooded fields being favourite feeding grounds, though saltmarsh plants are also taken. In some areas the grass is supplemented with stubble grain, potatoes, clover, and sprouting winter cereals.

Like greylag and pinkfoot, the whitefront is chiefly a day feeder unless greatly disturbed and may even roost on the feeding ground if

In snowy conditions the pigeon shooter sometimes resorts to white clothing for camouflage.

unmolested. It usually flies in to feed at daybreak or soon after and leaves at dusk but does not feed all day long and sometimes feeds under the moon, after which it usually flights to the shore for sand to aid digestion.

Less gregarious than the other grey geese, the whitefront often occurs in small parties or pairs. New arrivals are unsettled and, although they mix with greylags and pinkfeet, it is not until winter sets in that their flighting is at all predictable. Then those birds on estuaries move with the tide, flighting to inland marshes and fields at high water. At freshwater roosts they usually sleep on the margins rather than the water.

Whitefronts fly superbly and provide excellent sport. Like the other grey geese, they have deceptively fast, direct, and powerful flight, but are even more adept on the wing. If pressed they can take off almost vertically with a sudden spring. Flight is less heavy than the greylag's and more often in v formation. Their whiffling (spiral diving with wings half-folded) from height towards the feeding grounds is more dramatic than that of the greylag. Yet they remain very alert and if necessary will 'reverse engines' impressively to take them rapidly out of range after coming almost to a dead stop.

# THE WOODPIGEON

Every year in Britain many millions of woodpigeons are shot to protect farm crops, but fortuitously this provides excellent shooting at very low cost. Indeed there are many thousands of men who shoot little else, thoroughly enjoying the varied sport this alert and elusive quarry provides the year round. It is indeed our worst avian pest and the pigeon shooter gets most of his sport under the guise of crop protection, but secretly all shooters hope the grey hordes will continue undiminished.

In Britain the woodpigeon is very widespread, occurring in all but the most isolated and remote agricultural areas, though it is scarce on the higher Scottish hills, in the Outer Hebrides, and in Shetland. Numbers are much smaller in wetter areas such as Northern Ireland, where the concentration is on dairy farming. Grain-growing areas of the South-East are now the greatest attraction. The original deciduous woodland habitat is still used for nesting, but otherwise most woodpigeons spend their lives on farmland.

At long range the woodpigeon's best field mark is the white wing-bar but at close range the white patch on each side of the neck and black tip to the long tail are often distinct. The sexes are alike, though the female is fractionally duller and smaller. Juveniles look like dull adults, lacking the iridescence. The white neck 'ring' (hence the old name 'ring dove') starts to appear at about two months and is complete within about a fortnight. The young bird's irides are nearly

black but those of the adult are brilliant yellow. Its breast is particularly plump, skin pale, beak disproportionately large, thighs relatively thin, legs pinky-orange without scales, and claws pinkish, whereas the adult has purplish-red legs and toes and dark-brown claws. The plumage is complete after the first moult but continues to develop intensity of colour. The average length is 16 in and the average weight 1 lb 3½ oz for the male and 1 lb 3 oz for the female.

The woodpigeon's soft, far-carrying *coooo-coo, coo-coo, coo* is one of the most familiar sounds of summer. It is heard mostly from early spring to September and there are several variations, including what sounds at close range like a sigh. The species is most vocal in its roost soon after dawn and just before bedding down for the night.

Most nests are in trees—both deciduous and coniferous—and tall hedges, but in areas where few trees exist they occur in tall heather and, exceptionally, actually on the ground. They probably pair for life and nest in the same area each year where disturbance is minimal. The female builds the thin but conspicuous platform of twigs from material gathered by the male. Rarely high up, it is often only a few feet from the ground in undisturbed areas.

Two or three clutches of two (sometimes one or three) white eggs are laid, with a peak from July to September on farmland, so that hatching coincides with the main harvests—both wild and cultivated. However, eggs have been found in every month of the year. The seventeen-day incubation is by both sexes and the young are fed on the highly nutritious, cheesy 'milk' regurgitated from the crops of both parents. A single parent is quite capable of tending the squabs alone should its mate be shot. The young are fed for twenty-nine to thirty-five days before fledging.

A highly adaptable bird, the woodpigeon eats the equivalent of its own weight every four days. From January to March main foods include clover, lucerne, sainfoin, weed seeds, leaves of winter corn, holly berries, ivy berries, and frosted potatoes. Green crops such as rape, kale, sprouts, and cabbage increasingly come under attack during very cold weather. Much damage is done as even plants with only their tops pecked out have no commercial value.

In spring and early summer attention switches to newly sown grain (unearthed and sprouting as well as surface), peas, beans, maize, charlock, wild mustard, clover, rape, sprouting kale, turnips, and mustard.

During late summer ripe and ripening grain 'laid' by wind and rain is a major attraction alongside young kale, clover, mustard, grass seeds, ripe peas, woodland and hedgerow leaves and soft fruit.

Spilt grain brings many birds to the stubbles of autumn and early winter, but as this is ploughed in, clover becomes more important and slugs, worms, and ripe maize add variety. In December sugar beet fragments are an attraction in harvested fields which have not been ploughed. And the very elastic crop can hold a surprisingly large number of acorns or beech nuts.

Although the woodpigeon generally has three main feeding periods—soon after dawn, around midday, and late afternoon—when food is plentiful there is considerable seasonal variation and the shooter must study local patterns very carefully, especially as some foods take longer to digest than others. In high summer there may be a fourth feed late in the afternoon and in midwinter birds may even continue feeding for a short time after dark in order to gain sufficient energy from vegetable foods generally low in calorific value. Without local knowledge of what and when the birds are eating, it is a waste of time buying pigeon shooting, as an increasing number of desperate Guns do in reply to advertisements.

When determining the flightline prior to setting up a hide (if natural cover is insufficient) it is worth remembering that with such a generally dry diet the woodpigeon needs to drink frequently. Thus standing water, even that in a cattle trough, can be a major attraction and for you a better focal point than a huge feeding area. Also the birds prefer to feed out of the wind in a fold or dip in the ground and in drier situations to avoid the feet becoming 'balled up' with mud.

In between feeds the pigeon resorts to a 'sitty' tree where it can perch quietly to digest its food. Generally large numbers sit together and create another good focus for shooting.

Britain has a breeding stock of three to five million pairs, but the population probably doubles by the end of September and then gradually falls through winter. These resident birds are joined by a variable number of passage migrants and winter visitors from October on, especially when the whole of North-West Europe and Scandinavia are in the grip of severe cold. Then the flocks become progressively bolder and readily attack crops near houses.

Much has been written about the woodpigeon's changing behaviour in response to new cropping regimes and increased shooting in recent years. Yet the species has always been a difficult bird to shoot and there is never any excuse for foregoing thorough local reconnaissance. Whether decoying in the open fields or roost-shooting the woods, the pigeon shooter must remain highly mobile. So-called pigeon 'shyness' probably has more to do with an increasingly greater choice and quantity of food throughout the year than over-shooting.

Roost shooting is best in February, when the pheasant-shooting season is over, keepers need not fret over excessive disturbance of their birds in the coverts, and the big flocks have not yet dispersed to breed. Unless the aim is to drive all the pigeons away, shooting should stop while birds are still coming in, to ensure that the site continues to be used and pheasants are able to get up to their roosts safely.

# GROUND GAME

Four-legged or furred quarry are generally known as 'ground game'. Some, such as fox and squirrel, are commonly shot as pests, but in Britain the sporting shotgunner is concerned with only two species—hare and rabbit, both of which have always been important to pot-hunters.

## *HARE*

Many people have stopped shooting hares altogether in recent years as local populations have declined so much, probably mainly through the wider use of poisons in agriculture as well as habitat alteration and disturbance. But the distribution of the brown hare has always been patchy and areas remain where the animal is sufficiently concentrated to warrant continuation of the traditional special hare shoots held soon after the end of the gamebird-shooting season, in the belief that the species is a significant agricultural pest.

When large, open fields are driven, the fleet-footed brown hare offers good sport, but a typical line of Guns includes men who shoot only rarely and are not aware of the importance of safety in this activity. Walked-up hares generate fair sport too, though many British roughshooters are put off by having to carry the 8 lb-plus animal, unlike Continental Guns, who prize the hare above most other quarry.

It is not widely appreciated that the large hare population we had before the great decline after 1960 was but a relatively recent phenomenon. Towards the end of the nineteenth century there were even fears for the species' extinction, but enlargement of fields, removal of woodland, and ploughing-up of much more land helped it to thrive once more. The brown hare has a definite dislike of pastures with livestock, but woodland and hedgerows are used more for daytime resting than was previously supposed.

The brown hare is distinguished from the rabbit by its longer, black-tipped ears and its longer legs and loping gait. It differs from the smaller mountain or blue hare in summer by its brighter, yellow-brown colour and dark upper surface of the tail as well as its longer ears; in winter the mountain hare is white or has a transitional coat.

In Britain the brown hare is widespread on low ground, especially in the drier, arable areas of the south-east but is absent as a native species in Ireland, and the Hebrides and Shetlands, and missing from parts of north-west Scotland. Most introductions, including that to Ireland, have been largely unsuccessful.

The mountain hare is native to Ireland and the Scottish Highlands and is most numerous on grouse moors in north-east Scotland, where heather management for grouse favours hares too. The Scottish lowlands and the Pennine areas of south Yorkshire and Derbyshire

Following protracted population decline in most areas, brown hares are generally shot in only small numbers today.

# SHOOTING
# DAYS

It is, of course, a cliché to say that being there is enough. Yet outside shooting there can be a few areas of human activity in which this is more true. Days of big-bag obsession are long gone and today's sporting Gun is a hunter of peace, atmosphere, colour and adventure as well as quarry. His choice is wide, ranging across every habitat through all weathers, and despite increasingly restrictive legislation there is still a quarry for every season. And even in the pursuit of a single species there are days of incredible variety, each bringing its own great satisfaction and treasured memories. In this section I describe some typical forays.

# TASTE OF THE WILD

Few people who take up quarry shooting ever abandon it entirely. Most become hooked for life, enjoying hundreds of outings which they religiously record in cherished gamebooks over the decades, while others are content with only the occasional foray, relying on this safety valve to rid themselves of the choking fumes of modern life. It is a wonderfully refreshing way to enjoy what remains of our natural heritage while at the same time experiencing adventure and uncertainty in our otherwise very structured society. And it has forms and days to suit every character, from recluse and pot-hunter to naturalist and socialite. It's in the blood of all men, uniting town and country folk in great traditions, bringing colour and atmosphere and stimulating our neglected senses.

For the all-round British Shot, the sporting year begins at the end of July when so many of us descend on the Country Landowners Association's annual Game Fair to celebrate the riches ahead. Then the pregnant countryside is poised to deliver its wild harvest and the greatest variety of sport scents every wind.

An early and bounteous harvest in some quarters will bring good pigeon bags to stubble decoys, and what sheer delight it is to drop one of those grey-and-white foragers in a plume of feathers above the wheat. In early August the hot grain fields almost groan with relief as the remaining crop is lifted. And even as the combines advance—on the largest fields like a line of monstrous beaters—the woodpigeons fearlessly gobble up the spilt grain.

The woods are still lush in full Lincoln green and there is much fun to be had walking the edges where concealed, resting pigeon allow close enough approach for excellent snap-shooting. With a crack of startled pinions, the ring dove bursts from his sylvan solace better than any clay target. Sometimes he will unobligingly depart into the interior, thus denying you a shot, but more often than not out he comes with the panache of a Grand Prix winner, jinking and cornering to present a fine going-away shot.

Inevitably your summer-jaded reactions fail to claim the first bird, but even before you can replace the spent cartridge more birds scatter above you, disturbed by the shot but not knowing from whence it originated. Their starburst confuses you but composure returns just in time to take a long half-crosser. It is quite dead and the eager dog delivers it perfectly to your hand.

Eagerly you pop the warm bird into the gamebag net, snap the breech shut, and set off with a new spring in your step. Now you have that magic first bird. Now you savour some recompense for the early start and heightened senses enjoy the whole country scene all the more. The same new-found alertness which enables you to kill the next pigeon with controlled ease also enables you precisely to identify

*Previous pages* A pigeon retrieved: just part of the colour and atmosphere the modern shooter can expect.

the butterflies and birds dancing and diving about you, those same creatures which hitherto languished in the haze of your vagueness.

But all too soon the last corn is bagged, the pigeons have become more elusive, and the battle-scarred bale hide is damp and deserted in autumn mist. It is time for duck.

Last week, when you traipsed home with a couple of rabbits slung on your belt and the sun was a red giant behind the copse, you glimpsed a few shadowy mallard whickering into the stubbles. Here should be some fine sport in the days to come.

There are few partridges on your shoot this year and the small bag will be more worthy in October, so now you lay plans for 1 September on the foreshore. Deep down you know that the saltmarsh will be bathed in Indian-summer sunshine on a windless day when the air is thick with midges and the redshank will laugh at your optimism. Yet go you must. Back to the mire, the gurgling creeks, and the rising fish. Back to the spartina, the wavelets lapping against moored rowboats, and the floodtide of memories.

If 1 September should bring a good duck it will be a bonus. You will be there anyway, in obedience to the primeval hunter, instinctively following the migratory flocks. This day will be a mere appetizer, a stimulation of adrenalin and a stirring of blood in preparation for the wigeon which will give you such excitement on a wild winter's day.

Already time is at a premium. Your moor escaped the worst of the weather back in the breeding season and you must go north more often to keep the head of grouse to a healthy level. But each round-trip takes the best part of three days.

October is easier and there is a chance to enjoy those dream partridges. Not enough for a big driven day, but certainly the nucleus of a few walked-up outings with a handful of good chums. Then there is real colour in the countryside when garlands and bunches of red and orange berries bejewel every hedgerow and leaves are tinged with the same rufous tints we admire in partridge feathers. Yet there is time to educate the young pheasants and to remind them of their role in life. There are some good, seasoned birds to be taken in October and a little 'hedgerow bashing' will both sharpen us up and help lay plans for November's mighty gameshooting climax, when the great woods will echo to main days.

Thus gently we descend through December's pleasant brew of mixed and modest pheasant days laced with well-chosen coastal excursions, just catching our breath before Boxing Day's explosion.

Onwards then to those bracing days of deep frost and January's curling cock pheasants. But when winter has lain waste the land and most men doze contentedly, curled before the blazing hearth with a dram of malt, the true sporting adventurer is locked into some God-forsaken frozen waste after the geese.

All this plus woodcock, golden plover, snipe, hare, rabbit . . . .

127

# PHEASANTS FOR EVERYMAN –
# A DAY WITH THE LONGTAILS

Modern British gameshooting is firmly based on the cult of the pheasant, the 'longtail' which once played second fiddle to the abundant grey partridge. In due season, this colourful bird decorates every high street butcher's window, reflecting the sport's remarkable growth in recent years. In the general rush to 'get back to Nature' and sample traditional pursuits, pheasant shooting attracts men from all walks of life and anyone with the ready cash can buy his way in.

Many people get their first driven day through a friend in a syndicate, either taking his gun when he cannot make it or accompanying him on a special guest-Gun day. Or it could be that his contribution to the shoot is enough to enable him to have regular guests in addition to his own days. Perhaps he is the owner of the land, who has retained two or more 'guns' as part payment by the syndicate. But whatever the reason, if you are a beginner it is unlikely that you will know many of the other Guns.

On the day before the shoot, while you check over the points on safety and etiquette outlined in Chapters 4 and 5, the shoot captain will have finalized plans with the keeper. Allowance will have been made for forecast wind and weather, the desired bag and the capabilities of guests, and stand markers placed accordingly. Hopefully, if you are a beginner, you will have had sufficient notice to enable you to obtain suitable cartridges and to make sure you have wet-weather clothing available.

If you are not familiar with the shoot's location, make certain you have precise directions, and even then allow plenty of time for mistakes. Some people's estimations of distance and ideas of what constitutes a road suitable for saloon cars are abysmal, while others have a warped sense of humour and delight in seeing you bogged down to the axles. When you are out in the sticks things much worse than a puncture can impede your progress. Being stuck behind cattle or sheep in a narrow lane may delay you for a mere five minutes, but an impassable, flooded road may need a twenty-mile detour. On no account drive into the water without sounding out the depth first.

You will have discovered whether or not to take your own lunch. Generally, if it is a big, smart shoot there will be a substantial, hot meal in some convenient building, but on less formal occasions your own snack might suffice, with a promise of supper at the end of the day. However, I am often amazed at what some people regard as a snack. It can be very embarrassing to misjudge the occasion and pull out a Thermos flask and a small, plastic box containing a curled cheese sandwich, a piece of cake, and an apple, when all around you are Fortnum and Mason hampers brimming with caviare, game pies, and champagne.

Another successful drive. Today anyone with the ready cash can buy his way into pheasant shooting.

The expected bag and the number of cartridges required may be uncertain, so always have plenty of ammunition in the car. If you have a true friend who has been prepared to give up good sport on your behalf you could be in for some real action. But if you were invited very late or only because the first or even second choice guest could not make it then there are grounds for pessimism, especially late in the season when bags are generally smaller. However, over the years you are likely to have just as many unexpectedly good days as disappointing ones in terms of bags.

Assuming you are on time (five minutes beforehand is ideal), get introduced promptly by your caring host and as long as you do not have two heads or an orange anorak with a ban the bomb symbol emblazoned on it, some of the other Guns should at least try to engage you in conversation.

You will be reminded by your host or the shoot captain at the beginning of the day of all the usual safety rules: no low birds, etc., but also be warned of potentially dangerous drives where there is undulating ground—a great hazard in wooded country where beaters, stops, and neighbouring Guns cannot be seen. Listen carefully to everything he tells you and if in any doubt, always ask. Inevitably, there will be some Guns who are not paying enough attention and end up guessing when you ask them for advice, so always go to the 'boss' if you have a query during the day's sport.

The day's plans should always be described: how many drives you hope to have, their likely order, when and where you hope to stop for lunch, when you hope to finish, and so on. This may be boring for regulars when there is little change to the routine, but there is nothing worse than bumbling along on a strange shoot without any idea of what is going on. In any case, it adds greatly to the day's enjoyment if you understand the order and direction of drives, how some are interdependent and how the beaters are lined out. And if there is any change of plan during the day all the Guns should be told at the earliest opportunity. There has been more than one occasion when the Guns were facing the wrong way when the birds came over!

There may well be drives in thick woodland where you cannot see anyone else at all, not even neighbouring Guns, and then it is more important than ever that you are aware of the signals to start and stop shooting. Quite apart from safety considerations, you need to know when to be fully alert and when to vacate the position to be at the next stand on time.

When the address is over the Guns will draw for positions and if you are a guest it is likely that you will be approached first. Memorize the number and hand it back to your host. Practices vary, but it is common for number one to be on the right and number eight on the left, moving up two or three pegs at each drive. Your number will be clearly marked on a stick at each stand, but there may also be one or more walking Guns who accompany the beaters, act as flankers, and generally shoot only those birds which do not go forward to the standing Guns. If this is so your turn will come, but do not worry as the keeper or senior beater in charge of the line will try to make sure you are in the best place. Sometimes you will be asked to walk in line with or just behind the beaters but stop when you reach your numbered stand, where there is likely to be the chance of a few shots towards the very end of the drive.

Regulars will know which are the best numbers to have on each established drive, and on a shoot which has few good drives the guest could be very unlucky all day. However, the attentive host will be aware of this and may 'arrange' for you to have a good draw. He might well be quite open about this and come to you first, suggesting a certain number by pushing it slightly forward of the others. Sometimes the regulars will have been briefed that a certain number is to be left for the lucky guest.

Some shoots do not draw for pegs at all, but that is mostly on private shoots where the host personally places the Guns on each drive to ensure that everyone sees some action. However, this does enable the eccentric autocrat to have some fun and games with his guests.

Once you are at the first stand get yourself organized quickly as there is no knowing how soon the action will begin. Place your cartridge bag on the ground and take the gun from its slip. If you have been invited to use two guns you will have a loader with you and you should have practised changing guns beforehand. Naturally, the two guns should be a matched pair if your performance is to be at all smooth. Do not use a borrowed gun simply because you believe that your own is not good enough for the occasion. This will inevitably spoil your aim. As long as your gun is in good, safe condition its value does not matter in caring company.

If it is warm enough and it makes you more comfortable, you might take off your topcoat, but always keep your hat on when facing the sun. This is the moment you have been waiting for ever since the invitation arrived. It is a moment charged with anticipation and one to savour with the whole glorious day before you.

Behind you stand the attentive pickers-up, the breath of their labradors and golden retrievers billowing out into the frosty air. Cheerfully you wave to them to acknowledge their position, for they will be unfamiliar with your safety standards.

A horn or whistle sounds the start of the drive and you drop two bright cartridges into the chambers, the crisp, metallic sound of the closing breech echoing down the ride. Now you are on your own.

For a few moments there is silence, and you make a mental note of safe firing angles and what area constitutes your 'territory', at the same time hoping your neighbours will not be greedy.

Pheasant shooting – "on and
on he comes with all the
majesty of Concorde".

A robin's sweet carol drifts down from a nearby oak and you turn dreamily to admire the autumn colours about him. But almost immediately your attention is caught by the tapping of the stops, unseen in secret corners where pheasants are likely to run out the sides of the drive. You make a note not to shoot anywhere near them.

Your gun is held at the ready, safely pointing skywards. Then you glance sideways and see how relaxed your neighbour is. Obviously he knows there is yet some time to wait, so you casually lower your gun and place it over the crook of your arm, barrels pointing safely at the earth. But almost immediately a little muntjac deer scampers out and you are brought smartly to attention. It is the first one you have seen—a good talking point for later, when you will learn how common they have become. You are surprised that the deer is fleeing so far ahead of the beaters, who you have not yet heard.

Suddenly a pigeon bursts upon the scene and you wonder whether to shoot at it. Wisely, you decide not to in case you are accused of spoiling the drive, even though your neighbour is tracking the bird with great interest. Later you may discover that pigeons and crows are always shot, but better safe than sorry. You did not want to ask about them at the briefing for fear of being thought petty-minded.

Now at last you can hear the beaters, surprisingly close as they march uphill and over a rise. While they were in the valley you did not hear their urging and brush-bashing, but now there is no doubt they are coming your way and your heart beats faster and faster. Will you be in the 'pound seat' or will you even get a shot?

On they come, steadily drawing nearer, investigating every scrap of cover for skulking birds, their springer spaniels and terriers rushing about excitedly while the keeper growls at them through the trees: 'Hold back on the right . . . steady lads . . . Whose bloody dog is that?' He is understandably concerned that one or two of the unruly dogs will cause the bunching birds to flush as one, like a box of fireworks going off in every direction—the last thing required. What you want is a good, steady stream of birds going forward from a well-controlled line. But you are at the mercy of the keeper's and beaters' experience and commonsense.

A rabbit bursts from cover, but luckily it is closer to your neighbour, for you are worried about shooting one with so many people around. He lets it run safely though the line and spins to fire, but misses handsomely as it dives into cover. Secretly you are pleased because now you know that he is not a crack Shot.

Then a tawny owl floats over—a fairly common sight on a driven shoot. You automatically flinch at the movement but steady up rapidly lest your neighbour fears you might shoot the protected bird. The owl drifts away nonchalantly as if well used to the disturbance.

But now the excitement really mounts for there running through the undergrowth are the first pheasants. The craftier ones curl back to

test the walking Guns, but now comes the cry 'Forrrrward' and a cock longtail in its full glory decides that the path to freedom is straight over your inexperienced head. On and on he comes, scalding and chortling, larger and larger, small, whirring wings suddenly frozen as he glides powerfully with all the majesty of Concorde. Is he too low? Surely you cannot miss. Moments of indecision. He must be yours.

The gun comes sweetly to your shoulder and you follow through, pulling the trigger in textbook fashion. 'Hit 'im in the beak', they said. 'Come up through him, blot him out with the muzzle and fire, but you must keep swinging. Simple.' Then why have you missed so cleanly? Not one feather drops in consolation and you have left it too late for a second shot. All you can do is stare at the bird intently, wishing it would drop, trying to convince any onlookers that it must be hit—a 'runner' surely? But truthfully you have no real reason to suspect a pricked bird and must not be tempted to waste the time of the pickers-up, who are rarely fooled. They have seen it all before and know every sign of a wounded bird. Yet if you persist with your claim the diplomatic picker-up will probably pretend to go in full search, soon returning with another bird to save your embarrassment. But do this too often and you will be marked as a bad Sport.

No time for an inquest. Two more missiles are launched in your direction and, horror of horrors, you realize that you have forgotten to reload. But there is just enough time to replace the spent case and in a surprising patch of calmness you drop both birds stone dead—one at your feet, the other crashing into the rhododendrons behind a picker-up who calls out 'Good shot'. Now you are flushed with pride and satisfaction. Your blood is up and you even remember to reload.

A hen approaches, almost unnoticed, but suddenly veers away as if aware of your new-found skill. She swoops down over a little glade but the land agent on distant peg six has her number and the bird's head snaps back even before you hear the shot. Only a puff of feathers remains in the air as the pheasant's impetus carries it a further twenty yards before it bounces dead on the hard turf among the frozen molehills.

Another cock approaches, but it is too low and you have no hesitation in letting it pass. You are all keyed up and ready for anything. But before you have the chance to show your skill once more, the horn sounds the end of the drive and, reluctantly, you must unload.

The land agent sends his own dog for the hen as it is very close and, to your great surprise, a picker-up comes over with the cock you thought you had missed. It was a 'dropper'—one of those apparently untouched birds which has a fatal pellet in the heart or lungs and suddenly drops dead perhaps a quarter of a mile or so behind the line. Well used to such birds, the picker-up had positioned himself with a good vantage point.

You slip the gun into its sleeve and walk up the ride to meet the other Guns, some of whom appear clutching pheasants, while others run their dogs for unpicked birds. Those without dogs have carefully noted the positions of birds which have fallen in cover to make the work of the pickers-up much easier.

Already an hour has passed since the 9 a.m. start and you are keen to get on. But no one else is in a hurry, the sun is already melting the frost, and it is a great treat to be away from the office. The long wait on the first drive had been due to a 'blanking-in' manoeuvre, in which a few of the beaters had been sent on ahead to gather birds from adjoining hedgerows, bringing them back into the wood to be driven. They should have started earlier.

The second drive is some way off, so you all clamber aboard the shoot vehicle, an old single-decker bus. The sixteen beaters are already underway, a cheery bunch bumping up and down on their bale seats aboard a tractor-drawn trailer.

This time you are a walking Gun and the keeper suggests you keep about fifteen yards out in the field, fractionally ahead of the beaters in a big wood. Fortunately they are a good team, not too noisy and applying just enough pressure to keep the pheasants quietly scurrying on. Booming voices and rapid movement tend to make birds tuck up in cover, so that many of them flush too early and generally go in the wrong direction. The pheasant hates flying more than necessary as it soon drains its energy, so it is difficult to persuade it to make a long, straight flight more than once in an hour or so. With luck, the organizers will have borne this in mind when planning the day.

But now you are distracted by the plough underfoot, which is soft and slippery beneath the late-October frost and clings to your feet like lead plates. Hardly surprisingly then that you are totally off-balance when a woodcock breaks cover, so a good opportunity to bag this prized quarry is missed.

It is hard to see the beaters in the dense covert, especially when they move through a small spruce plantation, and you trust to your hearing to keep good position. But the men are well aware of where you are and obligingly one calls over, as quietly as possible, 'On the right'. And this time you have sufficient notice to get onto a super-charged hen that tries to fly out the back door. She is well hit, but a likely runner, so one of the men immediately puts his dog onto it. Whenever it is safe to do so, wounded birds should always be retrieved and despatched as soon as possible. It is distasteful to visit a shoot where winged birds are totally ignored until the end of a drive when there is no harm in gathering them immediately. And on the few occasions when all the dogs are already onto birds a Gun should stop shooting (again, as long as it is safe to do so) to put a nearby flapper out of pain. Sadly, many Guns are either too selfish or too embarrassed to do this.

135

As the second drive continues you hear some shots from the other two walking Guns—one in the centre of the beaters, the other on their left. Then comes a spattering of fire from the standing Guns as the most forward birds try their luck.

Another shot or two comes your way, but these are difficult, curling birds and you are glad there is no one nearby to see you miss. It will be bad enough later when you might have to account for the shots.

Now you reach your stand marker, where you must remain while the beaters work out the remainder of the drive. You are at the end of the wood and can see some of the other Guns lined out in the valley below.

The beaters are ordered to go very slowly now, inching forward to avoid a 'bouquet' of birds, for there are many here. You notice that some birds are still immature and short in the tail, but you also see that the Guns make no move against these 'squeakers', rightly leaving them for late in the season, when they will provide better sport. There is enough of a fusillade here anyway.

When you regroup in the valley you see that a good bag has been made and the game cart is called for. Both keeper and beaters brace up the birds with baler twine and suspend them in neat rows not too close together so that they cool quickly on the home-made trailer. Meanwhile, one of the Guns describes some of the more spectacular shots.

As the third drive gets underway the sky begins to cloud over and the whole scene is dulled. It is unfortunate that British weather is so unpredictable, for it often plays a crucial part in the success and pleasure of a shooting day, completely altering drives according to whether it is wet or dry. Birds avoid wet game crops, especially kale and other brassicae, which hold moisture for so long after even a single shower. And a bright morning after a wet night will entice pheasants away from woods where they have had to suffer incessant dripping. Thus crop drives are generally more productive in dry weather and in the morning and early afternoon.

On this day the wind gets up with the cloud and if it continues to increase could really call for some fine-tuning of the planned drives. Strong crosswinds are particularly troublesome, blowing the birds out of predicted line so that the Guns have to be moved or the angle of drive altered—not always possible. Where this is a common problem on exposed ground, keepers may peg a couple of extra places so that they can move the Guns up or down accordingly.

Later in the season snow will increase your appreciation of the countryside but may also affect the drives. A few inches can make things easier as it greatly reduces the birds' tendency to run so that stops become less important. And deep snow really helps the roughshooter as it makes birds squat more rather than charge off if they see anyone walking-up in the distance. But blizzard conditions may prevent the Guns even reaching the shoot and dense fog often

Driven pheasant shooting is now more popular than at any time in our history.

137

leads to postponement when it is unsafe to continue. Sadly, commercial shoots are often tempted to continue in unsuitable conditions to avoid losing a day's income.

However, such extremes are unlikely to bother you today. Your main problem now is that you have drawn a hot corner in full view of everyone and your performance is erratic. The joy of pulling down two 'screamers' is quickly overshadowed by missing four consecutive, relatively easy birds. Something must be done, so you rethink your coaching and determine to take the birds earlier, following through more deliberately, learning how that last-second, extra flip-on of the barrels often pays off. You can forget all about that 'Shoot at 'em' nonsense for anything but lowish birds and instead trust to your experience.

But there is another problem as this major drive has 'back Guns' too. Not only must you be sure to leave indifferent birds, as you would do normally, but you should also allow some of the moderate ones to pass, to increase their height or speed and give those men behind the chance of some fine birds. In any case they might 'wipe your eye' in killing some of the birds you miss. Back Guns are a must on some drives, but always easier to sort out on a private shoot where the host places the Guns. He will make sure that they are the very best Shots and perhaps take the opportunity to give himself a little shooting on a day when most of his time is taken up in making sure that his guests enjoy themselves.

Thus you are thrown in at the deep end, but at least you are aware of these considerations and at the end of the drive believe that your skill has been reasonable and, more importantly, that your behaviour has been impeccable. After all, you have already decided that you want to be invited again.

The drive is a great success and for the first time the old keeper smiles. Your friend is delighted that you have 'killed up' and you are pleased that you have not let him down.

Soon it is lunchtime and you are all very hungry, making short work of piping hot oxtail or cottage pie while the beaters have beer and sandwiches. There is plenty of wine, beer, and sherry to soothe your earnest conversation with a Gun who is concerned about fieldsports and politics and other endless heavy matters, but there is also a charming hostess who rescues you from the shoot bore with libations of brandy or port to accompany the magnificent Stilton. You are truly thawed. It is indeed a pleasant interlude and the atmosphere heady with cigars, but just as you are thinking that you must not overdo the drink your host declares that everyone must be on parade in five minutes, failing which he will cancel the next drive. It simply isn't on to keep the beaters waiting.

Back in the cold woods you have forgotten your number and wish that this was one of the shoots which issues cards at the beginning of the day, listing all the drives (usually named) with the appropriate stand numbers against each. This would also remind you of all those names you keep forgetting.

In the afternoon you remember to help the more elderly members of the shoot to negotiate obstacles such as ditches and fences, holding their guns where necessary. You also learn how useful 'sewelling' can be in woodland where only a ride denotes the shoot boundary and are thankful that you are not the one who has to keep the long string of plastic strips moving to dissuade birds from running away.

The rain holds off but the light fades quickly. There has been a good bag over eight drives and the organizers are not tempted to press on greedily while daylight remains. The birds must be given sufficient time to filter back from the fields and get safely up to their roosts before dark, when foxes are on the prowl.

It is over and you are sorry to see the close of play. The heavy cart creaks back to the cluster of old stone buildings where its load of 149 pheasants, six woodcock, four rabbits and two pigeons is hung in the game larder to await collection by the local gamedealer. Also shot were three magpies, two squirrels and two jays which are entered in the old gamebook under the quaint heading 'Various'. The Guns clean their weapons and the keeper pays the beaters and pickers-up, who disperse rapidly into all corners of the dusk.

You retire to the house for tea, whisky, and cake. Layers of cold, damp clothing are peeled off and left to steam over radiators while in another room the day is relived around a massive, crackling log fire. On the walls prints and paintings depict shooting days from long ago, when men of similar persuasion hunted the same quarry.

But now you are summoned to the porch, where the keeper has a fine, carefully selected brace of pheasants for you to take home. Thoughtfully, he also brings the woodcock which you were so pleased to shoot on the last drive, knowing that, like most other Guns, you will prize it beyond all else. The keeper's stern countenance has weathered more seasons than he cares to remember, yet once again he has done more than was required of him. For this character of the old school this truly is a way of life and no mere job. It is the least you can do to press a couple of ten-pound notes into his leathery palm as you shake his hand and thank him most sincerely for a memorable day.

It would be easy to get accustomed to such near-perfect outings, but over-indulgence might cause them to pall. Perhaps it is best that you cannot afford such sport all the time. Pheasant shooting has many faces and it is unfair to compare one with another, just as one cannot generalize in saying that wildfowling is better than pigeon shooting. All have their special attractions and it is not at all surprising that some of the richest men in Britain insist that they derive as much, if not more pleasure from walking-up hedgerows with close friends than they do from entertaining the high and mighty on a main covert day.

# AMONG THE COVEYS –
# THE CHARM OF PARTRIDGES

The indigenous grey partridge has never lost its great popularity among countrymen and sportsmen, but it has lost much of the traditional patchwork-quilt landscape which sustained it in great numbers up to the last war. Now there is a great effort to reinstate it and its superb sport is valued all the more. The introduction of the redlegged partridge is welcome, but small recompense for the widespread loss of the grey or English bird.

In Britain we shoot perhaps half a million partridges each year, compared with some twelve million pheasants, but rarely do they provide poor sport. With gameshooting now such a highly organized social activity, most partridges are now driven, but many people still eagerly seize the opportunity to walk-up coveys in the traditional way. The 'little brown birds' are particularly welcome on flat land where pheasants are difficult to launch to a sporting height.

However, partridges are much less predictable than pheasant and grouse, and on the partridge manor there must be constant review of drives according to crops and weather. It is little wonder that the good, specialist partridge keeper is worth his weight in gold.

Much of the attraction of partridge shooting is to do with the time of year it is carried out. Although its season is a month longer than that of pheasant shooting, it is undoubtedly more concentrated in the early months, when traditionally it fills a gap for the Gun who has everything between August grouse and the best November pheasants.

Overall, the best partridge shooting is in October, when late-developing birds are strong on the wing, they have all been over the Guns a few times, and there are still plenty left in favoured localities. Yet, as with wildfowling, there is a special attraction in September sport. For the man without access to grouse, September brings the first opportunity to resume gameshooting proper and when the weather is fine and warm, as in an Indian summer, there is a special charm. Waterproofs may be abandoned for cool cottons and a picnic beneath the hedgerow takes the place of a hot lunch behind closed doors. Idyllic days which traditionally draw the ladies into the field.

Generally, early-season partridge shooting is less hurried than pheasant shooting as the Guns have time on their side. With much more daylight in September and October, there is no panic to get all the drives in and ample opportunity to enjoy the gold of autumn before it fades. By the end of October, partridges cease to be of much importance for the man whose passion is walking around the hedgerows.

It has been said that in the old days, when partridges were so abundant, the Gun who walked them up became tired of endless

The partridge shooter thrives in a traditional patchwork quilt landscape and enjoys good sport well before pheasant shooting is in full swing.

140

going-away shots and was glad to see the end of the day. Driven shooting brought a greater variety of more difficult shots. This may be so, but there is also great satisfaction in working dogs to partridges and getting within range of the now very elusive coveys. This is also the finest way to explore and get to know the countryside, and you can be sure that if there are grey partridges present there will also be a wealth of wildlife. How fondly I remember all those meadows full of wild flowers and butterflies where the insect life was abundant and I could guarantee to find coveys of partridges right up to the early 1960s. Now all the wild corners are gone, the land is too manicured, and there is too much reliance on rearing and release.

Neither do we have much opportunity to walk-up the stubbles as the harvest is ever earlier and the fields ploughed-in as soon as possible in readiness for the next crop to stand through the winter. Fallow fields are a rarity in a hungry world obsessed with maximum profits.

But you will find partridges in root crops, especially swedes, which seem to harbour so many insects. Walking the long, straight rows of potatoes and sugar beet can also be productive and is a good way of covering the ground methodically, but bags will be much higher with good hunting dogs.

When a covey springs there is no warning at all and you must be quick to select a target as these whirring bumblebee birds scatter in all directions, chirruping in alarm. To get two shots off requires great concentration and considerable practice as you stumble about the roots, inevitably off-balance. The golden rule is to shoot the first bird you see. Try to switch targets and the covey will be down in cover or out of range before you can say Eley.

You must be fit for such sport, but at the end of the day your cheeks will glow, your heart will be pumping all the stronger, and hopefully you will have one of Britain's finest meals in your gamebag. Never, never pass the opportunity to walk-up grey partridges. But do not waste your time in stomping after the redlegged or French partridge. The Frenchman is an incessant runner and much more suited to driving.

It is widely believed that a large team of beaters is essential for partridge driving, but this is not necessarily so. Sometimes three or four will suffice. But reconnaissance is important and it is necessary to establish the birds' preferred flightlines, for it will be easier to drive the partridges in these directions. Individual coveys have their home patches and sometimes it is fairly easy to predict where they will exit if you surprise them. The Guns can be placed accordingly, with walking Guns among the beaters to deal with the unexpected.

Perhaps because they are creatures of more open country, partridges are more vigilant than pheasants and it is important to keep noise to a minimum when shooting them, especially as the season progresses. Guns should be instructed to forget their small-talk for a while and approach stands quietly as the birds may be lurking nearby.

Cover is important too. Traditionally, the best partridge manors planted hedges specially to provide nest-sites and concealment from predators for the birds, as well as natural screens for the waiting Guns. And many of these hedges would be very high indeed to give flushed birds a good lift. But where cover is scant, as it is so often on the big, modern farm, not only is it very important to keep still and be soberly dressed but also to get behind a temporary screen of hurdles or bales. These must be erected three weeks beforehand to give the birds plenty of time to get used to them and firmly staked to prevent them toppling over.

When the great day comes, all your careful planning may be defeated by torrential rain that soaks the birds so badly that they refuse to fly and you have no choice but to cancel. However, a contrary wind may be dealt with by adjusting the beaters' line of approach and having some spare pegs to move the Guns along. The interdependence and frequency of the drives should not cause a problem as, unlike pheasants, partridges do not need a long rest before being flown a second time. On the contrary, return drives should always be carried out straight away as birds will start to walk home if you divert your attention elsewhere.

Partridge beaters often carry flags, especially the flankers, but these should not be waved continually. In turning birds, their main advantage is in surprise and therefore they should not be carried high over the shoulder to be seen by all the partridges in the area. The flags should be kept furled and low until the birds approach within 50-60 yards. Then they must be waved vigorously so that the startled birds turn back over the Guns.

With the weather still warm and muggy in September, shot partridges must be allowed to cool quickly and rapidly transferred to fly-proof larders or else they will not be fit for the table and no gamedealer will be interested.

The redlegged partridge is much easier to rear and to hold on ground than the grey, which is notorious for its wandering. It is also of some use in helping to break up coveys of driven greys so that birds come over the Guns in smaller numbers, target selection is easier, and sport more spread out.

Now more redlegs are reared and released than at any time in the past. The trend towards hand-rearing started in the south of England at the end of the 1960s and has increased almost thirty-fold since then. In East Anglia the upturn started a few years later but has proceeded at a much faster pace in a generally more suitable, drier habitat, and levels of rearing there are now sixty times as high as they were in the early seventies. The increases in the West Country and the north of England began in the early 1980s.

# GLORIOUS GROUSE

Grouse shooting really took off when access to northern moors became easier, in the nineteenth century, and the introduction of driving turned it into a social sport. Since then the 'king of gamebirds' has been unchallenged in gameshooting circles. It continues to attract wealthy sportsmen from home and abroad so that vast acreages are still set aside for its kingdom and much research continues into ways of maintaining supply to meet the ever-increasing demand.

Yet grouse shooting need not be terribly expensive. Large numbers of sportsmen still prefer the old-style walk-up, which may be had for a few tens of pounds and is equally exhilarating in the land of heather and misty mountains. The bags are inevitably small on such dogging days, but that is no bad thing in an age when too much emphasis has been placed on quantity rather than quality. The interest in walked-up grouse is keeping pace with demand for driven birds.

One of the most obvious attractions of grouse shooting is that it begins in warm and, hopefully, sunny August—on the 'Glorious Twelfth'. Not only does it provide the season's first opportunities for gameshooters to leave the grim worlds of commerce and industry far behind, but also the chance of a healthy holiday in idyllic surroundings. And today it is so well organized, with every facility on hand for those prepared to pay, that there is no reason why even the most delicate Guns should not take part. In the early season at least it is a suitable pursuit for the refined, as far removed from the mud and discomfort of wildfowling as the Earth is from the Moon.

Through its associations with wealth and privilege, grouse shooting has always been the target of class-conscious protest, yet today there is little discrimination on the moor. If you can pay you can take part as even the wealthiest landlords have gone commercial.

There are, of course, many similarities with pheasant shooting—the drawing for positions, the etiquette, good sportsmanship, tipping, etc., but there are also major differences. The red grouse is a thoroughly wild bird, not the subject of rearing and release schemes, and its behaviour makes it much more difficult to shoot than the average park-reared longtail. To come to terms with it you must be calm, and have good eyesight and well-co-ordinated reflexes, as well as skill with the gun. If you can take two birds out of a covey in front then you are doing very well indeed, and one in front and one behind is no mean achievement.

Later in the season the grouse shooter also has the elements to contend with: many of the moors are in areas of very high rainfall and in such exposed positions it does not take much of a blow to register a nasty wind-chill factor. Wet-weather clothing must always be to hand as the purple mountains leading ever onward may be shrouded in driving rain in an instant, and there is no place to hide. And if you are

Grouse shooting, with the purple mountains leading ever onward.

very unlucky indeed, the entire day may be cancelled through floods making the burns impassable to beaters. Many of the drives are interdependent and there is no point in continuing with them if you have not been able to gather birds in the beginning.

Moorland picnics can be very splendid affairs with the wicker baskets strewn across the ground and Guns stretched out beneath the wide blue yonder. But when a storm blows up from nowhere they can be very soggy indeed and if there is no building to hand there might be nothing for it but to squelch it out in the vehicles, hoping the downpour will pass. However, some established moors are very well catered for, with delightful stone huts which blend superbly with the surroundings.

Cover for the Gun is essential on the open moor as the grouse will not fly over man so readily as the pheasant will. Fortunately the grouse tend to follow the same paths around certain contours when flushed in particular directions and it is possible to build effective permanent butts. Indeed, some moors still make good use of butts erected in the nineteenth century. Where possible, they are sunk below ground level and generally have dry-stone walls topped with heather. Concealment is more important on longer drives off hill ground in Scotland, where large teams of beaters bring birds right off their territory into unknown country, where they will be more nervous.

Where the land is too flat for a half-sunk and drained butt, raised butts of wood or other suitable materials must be erected, though grouse soon get used to them and approach without fear if the Guns are well concealed. Sometimes you will also come across less substantial raised butts which are of an experimental nature, testing new drives, usually later in the season.

Most grouse are shot during the first five weeks of the season and the motto generally is to shoot hard and early as many of the grouse will die anyway through natural causes, though obviously allowance must be made for the year's productivity. Today, a good driven day is anything over a hundred brace and days of up to 400 brace are exceptional. A single Gun walking-up may tramp many miles, falling down pot holes and half-drowning in bogs for the sake of a single brace, but go home as happy with his day's shooting as the man with the fat cigar.

Twelve to twenty beaters are usually employed on a driven day, though some of the larger estates may need two teams and have more than thirty men on the hill at once. There are usually four to six drives during the day, each covering 500-2,000 acres or more. Most of the experienced beaters will be local shepherds, farmers, or keepers, supplemented by students on vacation.

As in partridge shooting, flankers are employed to funnel grouse back into a drive by showing themselves or waving flags at the critical moments. Only experienced men are entrusted with this important position as they can make or break a drive.

All the usual safety rules are particularly important in grouse shooting as adjacent butts are often at different levels and may even curve around a hill. Many estates provide two sticks to be stuck into the top of each butt to prevent any dangerous shooting along the line or at a flanker. You must never swing through the line but always point the muzzles skywards in turning to shoot behind at birds going away.

The speed of grouse is very deceptive: what appears as a speck on the horizon one moment will be a cannonball hurtling past you the next. Have a good idea of range before the drive begins (it may help to remember that butts are usually about fifty yards apart) and try to take the birds in front, remembering that a bird spotted will probably be at least twenty yards closer by the time you have pulled the trigger. Do not be tempted to turn and take birds going away when others are still coming in front.

If a pack comes over, you may be temporarily confused. As with partridges and duck appearing in quantity, always select the first bird which takes your eye and do not change your mind. If you are successful, make a mental note of the fallen bird's position before concentrating on the next as even your loader will probably be too busy to do this for you. Picking-up can be particularly exhausting in heather for both man and dog and it is important that you count and mark your birds as accurately as possible.

## THE MAGIC OF ROUGHSHOOTING

For the man who attaches more importance to enjoying the peace and quiet of the countryside than socializing with fellow Guns, the roughshoot is ideal. Some are shared by a group of kindred spirits, but even then there is no very organized and intensive rearing and release scheme or any great alteration of the habitat. The accent is on a very mixed bag in modest numbers—a natural and reasonable cull taken through walking-up rather than driving game over standing Guns.

A little judicious feeding will often increase the head of game and help prevent existing stock from wandering, though there is always the risk of being accused of legalized poaching when surrounded by estates where game is reared on a large scale. Much more important is pest and predator control, and in many cases the shooting of these forms an important part of the average day's sport. Yet this should always stop short of outright warfare.

Many roughshoots are very small indeed—perhaps only a few acres—and sandwiched between gardens or areas with public access. Yet it is surprising what sporting pleasure these little patches of wilderness can bring, with each oasis of habitat regularly attracting specific quarry. For example, snipe love those oozy corners in

low-lying fields where water often stands for months on end, encouraging rushes and reeds. Duck too will flock in where enough open water is available.

I always enjoy the excellent camaraderie of a formal, driven shooting day, whether of the wise-cracking, barn-sandwiches type or the genteel pass-the-port-at-the-manor variety. But there is no denying the sheer exhilaration of a roughshoot, especially in icy midwinter when the exercise alone is welcome. Assuming you have a patch where variety of habitat still exists in this increasingly uniform countryside, there is no reason why your gamebag should not be full. Apart from the usual wily cock pheasants on very welcome lengthening late-January days, wildfowl are on the move, pigeon roosts have built up, and rabbiting is at its best.

Walking about after such quarry is also the best way to learn about nature in its teeming variety. And at the end of each outing, apart from some fine, healthy meals in the bag, there is that wonderful feeling of fulfilment and a bursting desire to recount every detail to family or friends with sympathetic ears. Failing these there is always a diary or gamebook.

When idling alone with the gun there is usually a better chance for mallard, teal, and snipe if unaccompanied by a dog, for then there are fewer shots at pheasant, rabbit, and hare and the best spots are more likely to be approached with silence and caution. And this is where familiarity with your area is so important. If a teal is hoped for at Silent Pool then the expected hare at Windy Corner must be ignored. If woodcock is to feature on the menu then 'Cock Bottom must be approached with stealth and no warning shot let off at the inevitable longtails in nearby Barker's Copse.

The more you shoot alone the wiser you become and a kind of in-built priority develops. Without any planning at all you know how best to find and bag each quarry, yet at the same time there is the thrill of the unexpected, such as a fall of woodcock in exceptional weather.

Although the driven game shooter may look down on the roughshooter, the latter needs greater all-round skills as generally he has far fewer shots to perfect his marksmanship with. And whereas the standing Gun specializes in those few species of game which can be gathered and brought to him in reasonable numbers, the walkabout roughshooter must have considerable fieldcraft to find and outwit a wide variety of quarry.

As the season progresses, the roughshooter's task gets even harder. If he shoots, say, once a week, by November the partridges are well aware of what constitutes danger and there are few birds more cunning than a cock pheasant which has been hunted up a hedgerow and missed once or twice. Even wilder birds such as duck and snipe rapidly learn the lesson of gunfire and present few opportunities

The walkabout roughshoot provides great variety and is an excellent way to discover more about the countryside.

149

towards the end of the season. Yet for most driven shooters the size of the bag is restricted only by the extent of the rearing programme, the number of birds left on the ground, and skill with a gun. However, it must be admitted that in the majority of cases the driven bird is flying much faster than that walked-up and is therefore a harder mark unless obscured by cover.

The roughshooter must also be a good dog man, whereas the driven shooter can leave the dogwork to beaters and pickers-up while he concentrates on his accuracy. But even with the best dog the roughshooter cannot always be sure which direction his game will come from. Indeed, this is half the fun.

The driven shooter is often transported in comfort from stand to stand and has little to carry except his gun (sometimes not even that), but the roughshooter walks for hours through often dense undergrowth, carrying everything he needs for the day. And if he is successful the steadily increasing weight of game in his bag is a great handicap when taking further snap-shots. Many of these chances come only in thick cover, whereas the man on his peg usually has all the time in the world to consider whether a shot is 'on' and how best to take it.

There is no denying the immense satisfaction to be had from roughshooting alone. It is not simply wealth which determines whether you are a roughshooter or driven game man. Most people like a little of each, if only for variety. Indeed, I have known very rich men who have become so bored through having so much driven shooting they have almost given up the exercise and have turned to solo walkabouts for their amusement, thus recapturing all the excitement which they knew in their energetic youth. As in all pursuits, variety and quality are essential to lasting satisfaction.

I too remember the endless days of roughshooting when every aspect of the sport awaited my discovery and enthusiasm was not limited by aching bones or business schedules. Take, for example, the occasion when in my sapling youth I stepped out with my old double hammergun into the tail-end of a blizzard which brought an eerie light to the hour before dawn on New Year's Eve.

My jacket was heavy with junk, such as squashed toffees and string, but most carefully stashed were three Eley Grand Prix fives, one Hymax, and one Alphamax for really special shots. All these cartridges had paper cases. In those pocket-money days I always knew the precise number of cartridges in hand and every shot would be made to count.

The snow fizzled out just as I reached my shooting zone and immediately I dropped two fives into the chambers. At that period, when securing a meal was uppermost in my mind, I always preferred fives to sevens as the heavier shot seemed to be much better at toppling sitting pigeons at long range, especially when they were partly obscured by branches in their gloomy roosts. And there were certain haunts where it was virtually impossible to get within close range of the drowsy, yet surprisingly alert birds. With limited ammunition, certainty of killing was all-important.

Anyway, on this particular day a favourite oak was positively fat with pigeon—silhouetted fruits clustered in the cold. Even these suspicious birds could hardly have expected a visitor on such a bitter day and I was easily able to get within forty yards.

Quaking with cold and excitement, I aligned the bead sight with a bunch of six, half-afraid to cock the hammers lest the birds should hear. The thunder of my shot tore the stillness apart and the fug of gunsmoke hung about me in the icy air as just one pigeon fell heavily, bouncing from branch to branch and landing in a bush. But as the startled pack burst about me in grey confusion my second barrel fortuitously downed another two.

Never wasting a moment, I reloaded with the third number five in the half-choke barrel and the Hymax in the full-choke before searching for the birds, as I knew this might take some time in the deep snow. It is surprising how dead game seems to be swallowed up by deep, fresh snow, but hopefully there would be a few spots of blood or feathers to aid the search.

The first bird was soon picked from the blackthorn at the base of the oak, though I was well spiked by the bush in the process. Hardly had I started to flounder about after the others, toppling into drift-filled ditches and stumbling over hidden branches, when a big rabbit exploded from a few briars arched over the snow nearby.

The remaining Grand Prix five smashed a dead branch and spurted the snow as I missed a yard behind, but the dose of Hymax stopped bun proper and he wriggled his last right at the entrance to his burrow. Now I had something to keep my side warm.

There was only the Alphamax left and still to come was the saltmarsh—usually the highlight of my day. But I wanted a duck more than anything so quickly kissed the long-brassed cartridge good luck, placed it carefully in the full-choke barrel, and strode off. Now I was flushed with success and my toes throbbed with new-found heat after all the exercise.

I had missed any dawn flight, but remained highly optimistic as I nestled into the black bushes along the foreshore. The suffused sun sat on the horizon like a huge apricot and parties of curlew quartered the gleaming mud freshly exposed by the ebb tide. Action was never long in coming there on days of such cold. But with just once chance I would surely wait for a near certainty.

I could almost feel the whoosh as a pack of teal whistled past my frozen left ear, dipped as one into a deep creek, and were gone before I could swallow. The sun grew steadily stronger and I was entertained by the minuets of dancing waders.

A lone mallard quacked disconsolately along the main channel, way out of shot, but at last came the hallowed music I had been hoping for—the *whee-oo* of wigeon. It seemed like an eternity between first hearing their distant call and the magic moment when six silhouettes set their pinions to plane down in my direction.

But once again excitement spoiled my rhythm, and even as I squeezed the back trigger, discharging the mighty Alphamax load into the ether, I knew that I had missed. Oh well, I could hardly complain with my bag of pigeon and rabbit. And there was still plenty of time to race home, scrounge some more pocket money and get down to the gunshop, before it closed at lunchtime, to secure more cartridges for evening flight. Mother should be pleased with the rabbit.

I have many such happy memories, but conjuring them up invariably makes me long for the days when there was just that bit more wildness about the land and the roughshooter had little trouble in getting permission to range far and wide. Such mixed days are still by far the best way to introduce a youngster to shooting. There is no crowd to witness that high percentage of early misses, no time to stand around until anxiety spoils your aim, and no uncertainty over etiquette to ruin your concentration. But there is variety and an overwhelming sense of achievement in hunting and killing your own dinner.

## WILDFOWLING – THE GREAT ADVENTURE

Wildfowling is by far the most difficult and exacting branch of British quarry shooting, demanding great patience and physical and mental stamina, as well as knowledge of natural history, keen observation, and natural hunting skills. To the newcomer it offers frustration, pitiful bags, bone-cracking cold, and great danger, but should he have the character to persist in this great adventure he will discover treasures beyond price.

Of course, I am talking about the coastal shooting of wildfowl, though many shooters insist that wildfowling also includes the inland shooting of duck, geese, and waders. That too is a great sport, but for me at least it does not have the same zest as shooting below the sea-wall, where sea, sky, and saltmarsh envelop you in an ever-changing, mysterious wilderness.

But first let us take a look at inland wildfowling, which purists demote to 'duck shooting'. Admittedly it can be pretty tame, as when mallard are reared on stillwaters, but there are places where the wilder migratory fowl swing in on buffeting easterlies and then the challenge is really on. No one who shoots a circling mallard put off a fed lake can call himself a wildfowler, but perhaps one who tackles the wigeon and pintail on desolate fens and flashes and floods within sound of the surf is worthy of the title.

What about somewhere like the Ouse Washes, where there is little to stop winds all the way from Siberia? Here too you need total disregard for personal comfort. There is no tide to contend with, but it is quite easy to pitch headlong into a dyke or racing river, and there is certainly plenty of open space and sense of isolation. A truly fitting place in which to engage great packs of Russian wigeon or raiding parties of uncompromising teal.

Such wilds still demand the early raiding party, the stumbling through darkness and flood, and a search for a good position on the frozen wastes, always with the chance of crashing through the ice and flirting with frostbite. But there is more reliance on hides and decoys and a greater feeling of security than our saltmarsh man ever knows. Geese can be drawn too but no one could claim that a decoyed, inland goose has anything like the magic of one driving into a gale over the breakers. I have shot both in fine style yet found no comparison.

But there is another side to inland fowling—September stubblers. Shooting mallard and teal, and sometimes other species, on corn stubbles is excellent fun. There is no wild location, but the quarry is certainly wild and there are some marvellous sunsets to savour. And it provides a brush with the fowl at a time when coastal sport is rather tame.

Today, finding stubblers at the right time is not so easy as the harvest is ever earlier. But traditionally an early September start requires a few days' reconnaissance in late August: evenings spent scouring the quieter farms and gazing into the sunset for duck on the move. Pay particular attention to laid corn too, for duck prefer it to harvested stubbles where the gleaning is patchy.

But once you have found the 'in' field you must take advantage of it quickly and get permission to tackle it before the farmer completes his combining. Unfortunately, he often works late into the night as the dew at that time of year rises only just before dawn. Modern machines can easily deal with blown wheat and barley and all you can do is to pray for rain to keep the farmer from 'your' field.

Although duck will feed at any time, the best inland shooting of this type is at dusk and dawn when the birds are flighting in and out, not expecting to be disturbed. You must arrive early and hide on the flightline in the ditch or hedge nearest the feeding zone, so that you can intercept approaching birds. There should be plenty of natural cover at that time of year so you will not need a hide, as you would on the open washes. But you must have a good, clear view of the oncoming birds, especially as the light fades and even mosquitoes can look like quarry to strained eyes. A call such as the Olt 66 will be more useful than a few decoys, especially as the duck may be heard a surprisingly long way off.

Although many of these stubblers will be juveniles, which should be spared for better sport later on, they all learn quickly and will follow their leaders in circling your field a number of times before landing. True wildfowling it may not be, but what does that matter when the birds are sporting and wild and your surroundings so stimulating? You will see the sun set on a world truly at peace, shades of colour you never knew existed and, if you are very lucky, the phantom barn owl will drift by in his search for supper.

September is also a very soothing month on the coast and, although sport then cannot be compared with that of midwinter, fowlers always have that great urge to get down to the sea on opening day.

As soon as you top the sea-wall you know that you are home. The same old smells, bubbling mudflats, and lazy seagulls greet you as though you never left. There is the constant to-ing and fro-ing of wings, the easy rhythm of the tides, and a timelessness on civilization's neglected margin.

Sparkling channels soon swell again and the tall, summer salt grasses now energizing in bright sunlight will be as forests to the ranging mullet and bass. As you walk the mile along the sea-wall to your intended station for evening flight, a lone whinchat rises and drops before you. Within a few weeks he will be off to tropical Africa, but now he is a good companion of the wildfowler. And on a very soft mudflat two dozen bartailed godwits feed busily. These passage migrants and winter visitors are no longer on the quarry list.

With so much equipment to carry you get very warm and are relieved to reach your post. You are familiar with the usual flightline here and lose no time in building a hide of driftwood and seaweed, load up with number fives, and sit back to watch summer slip away.

Curlew and redshank tease, for they too are no longer on the quarry list, though the former remains so in Northern Ireland. In the dykes behind the sea-wall, feathers prove that duck still favour this quarter, but when will they come and which is the most likely direction?

Soon the brilliance has left the sky. The sun, though still at thirty degrees, is already orange and indistinct and the frieze of trees around the harbour fades into various tones of grey according to distance. Seagulls surround you but there is not a duck in sight.

Suddenly comes the first wave of mallard, but they quack over far too high; even a 4-bore will not touch them. The sun is much lower now and more distinct as the orange burns to gold. More mallard, but again they are too high, though they are on the right line. Now another four, this time to your left, but once again stratospheric: there is no wind to keep them down.

Gunfire rolls around the harbour; there is hope yet. At last that magic line at the right height, but alas they rise too soon and swing left in an uneven, black v right across the face of the sun. Mosquitoes continue to harass.

Another two flights, but the sky has no ceiling and the air is windless. You can look at the sun now without being dazzled—it is

quite red. A heron cruises over, assessing the day like a judge with hunched shoulders looking down from the bench. Out on the ooze, waders assemble before the advancing tide.

Before long the sun has disappeared behind low cloud. There is a muffled shot from the distance and a great congregation of waders moves up the harbour, each species seeking its own company. Now ten minutes of near silence. The mist is already thick over the low-lying fields behind the sea-wall and in wisps over the water. You are well bitten.

The light is still fairly good. A yacht, sails neatly stowed, heads for base. You cannot hear its motor. Three lapwings rise out of the sea mist to haunt you. Two more yachts come, this time much closer, crews cutting the engines momentarily to chatter as the yellow-lit masts and green-lit gunnels mark their progress home. Not even a teal comes to buzz the shoreline; only a bat and a number of large moths to delude and stir the nodding fowler. Nothing will come now so you pack up and follow the dog's nose back along the dark sea-wall. There will be another flight, and anyway the beer will be especially invigorating after all that fresh air and exercise. As on so many occasions, there is no bag, but you could say that being there was enough.

I live some forty miles inland but always feel the pull of the sea. When maple leaves fall as yellow stars on the damp ground I know that wildfowl are thronging about my favourite marshland haunts. When worm-casts pimple the soft lawn and the robin's song is deep in melancholy I know that the sun-worshippers have left the beach to God and Nature. When the mist never really clears the morning air and the quiet dusk is charged with the massing of starlings, I know that the first ripple of winter is moving along the coast. It is time, once again, to seek the wild duck between the tides.

The great, post-harvest pigeon flocks have been thinned and scattered, flapper duck are now substituting muscle for fat, and pheasant training is coming along nicely for the first big day in November. The richness and diversity remain, the sporting calendar is clearly defined in the language of outdoors and there is no need for the enthusiast to rely on the written word. The mysteries of migration are in his bones and, just like any predator lifting his head to scent the wind, he 'feels' when the time is right to pursue each quarry.

But in this world of specialization and relentless pursuit of material things few men have the time and opportunity to get to know the objects of our chase as well as they might wish. Most fowlers must content themselves with being 'hit-and-run' men—those unfortunate souls whose need to be gainfully employed by other men away from the marsh means poor attendance. And that is bad news, for no book is any substitute for learning fieldcraft the hard way—on

The wildfowler must have great patience and physical and mental stamina as well as natural hunting skills.

your own. It is all very well courting favour and advice from an old hand who knows his patch intimately, but to have everything laid on for you will not cultivate the adaptability and dogged determination essential to every wildfowler.

In most good clubs founded in prime areas there is a hardcore of members who approach the sport from a different angle, putting fowling first and the job last, with the family somewhere in between. These few old salts, who linger on the quay with their hand-rubbed baccy and endless commentary on the quality of life, seem to have all the time in the world and give the impression that not a wing stirs within a mile without their knowing it. But who are these sages and where did they come from?

Almost without exception, such stalwarts are descended from local families whose lives have turned entirely around the pattern of the tides and the rhythm of the seasons. Whether it is casual labour on the land, netting fish, rabbiting, taking trippers angling in summer, logging, coppicing, basket-making, stick-making, or a spot of building work cash-in-hand, they always seem to find a handful of coins for a 'jar' at the Dog and Duck. Employment is simply to 'keep the wolf from the door'—no more—and they are free from the obsession with ambition which plagues most of us. Their admirable philosophy and unhurried manner bring to the sport a relaxed approach which is hard to beat.

Our man of the marsh lives in a quaint little flint or stone cottage within sound of the surf. The salt air continually forces the paint from his windows and his garden is crammed with objects which are practical, yet hardly worth keeping. His door is never locked, his fire is hardly ever out, and there is always a welcome for the diplomatic at the hearth where his sea socks hang to dry.

He is always available—to show the way, suggest where bait might be dug, contradict weather forecasts, get the broken-down car back on the road, row you across to the island, produce a few fish for supper, and perhaps even act as guide for the novice fowler. But most important of all, he is always close by to take advantage of a sudden influx of quarry. And nothing is more conducive to satisfactory fowling, even today.

Writing in 1850, A.E. Knox of Sussex declared: 'The principal destruction of wildfowl in the British islands takes place on the coast during severe winters.' Today we would not use the term destruction but there is still a great deal of truth in Knox's statement. Yes, we have statutory severe-weather shooting restrictions, but they are not unduly repressive and certainly do not prevent our man of the marsh making good bags at opportune moments. Long before protracted frosts have attracted interest in the newspapers, he has been taking stock of the steady build-up of quarry and making good, but sensible bags according to local acceptability.

Contrast this with the lot of the unfortunate modern wildfowler. Forever in a rush, he is under constant pressure to make the most of his limited leisure time and, quite understandably, when a golden opportunity comes his way he wants to take it. He will have travelled a long distance at great expense, kitted himself out with guns and equipment which are regarded more as collectors' items than tools, and be powered by romanticism rather than realism. His heart may be in the right place but he is not very practical.

Our enthusiast's day begins at some God-forsaken hour in a temporarily quiet city where even the milkman is still snoring. An ill-chosen, insufficient snack thrown into his gamebag is matched only by the inadequacy of his clothing. He is tired, late with his preparations, in his wife's bad books because he cannot take her out for a picnic, and if he gets into position on the foreshore before first light it will be surprising. If he does not disturb Guns already settled in favoured spots it will be astonishing and if he returns home at a sociable hour with anything tangible to show for his efforts it will be a miracle. He has not done his homework and survives purely on determination.

Of course this is an unfair picture to paint of the average modern fowler, and the old, wise man of the marsh is a very rare bird indeed. Most people are somewhere between the two extremes and I never cease to be amazed at how easily satisfied most gunners are. Some go on for many years with only the occasional mallard or missed snap-shot at teal to sustain them. To outsiders this enthusiasm seems baffling.

But the fowler knows that there are treasures which cannot be brought home. On the drive down through dark lanes while fellow men slumber they take simple pleasure in seeing all the creatures of the night about their food-gathering. Owl, rabbit, and fox, caught in the headlights, provide stimulating, wild pictures to be remembered at day's weary end. Traffic-free roads are a delight to drive on and the peace of a countryside at rest is refreshing in itself.

On parking near the marsh, a lone curlew is heard to burble beneath the stars and there is a real buzz of excitement as Guns gather to discuss tactics. Whispered plans drift away on a bitter wind and when all are dispersed to dark pits of hope the only sounds remaining are the panting of the dog and the rustling of rats among the bushes.

Almost before the heartbeat has had time to settle, the magic which is denied most men begins with the plaintive cry of a peewit. Slowly, slowly another day dawns as if its magnificent orchestration has been entirely for your benefit. Such colour, such splendour and such mingling of bird cries and movement of untamed spirits. It is hard to believe that this would take place day in, day out regardless of any human witness. This is no special show. It is Nature in her everyday attire and poor are the men who fail to recognize her riches.

All too soon, dawn, duck, and sport (if any) reach a crescendo and before you can sigh, the explosion of life is over. All across the mudflats and all along the sea-wall, Guns ease cramped frames from scant hides, blink in the full light of morning, and splodge back across the mire. Some go duck in hand, others trail disappointment, but most will return to try their hands once again in this fascinating sport.

Back by the boatyard, at the end of the sea-wall, the old salt sits puffing his pipe. He knows where you went wrong or whether you were simply wasting your time. But there is a twinkle in his eye, an enthusiasm for the adventure of every new tide, and an undaunted spirit which wins our admiration. To take his place would be very satisfying indeed, but sadly there are few of us prepared to accept his view of creature comforts for longer than a day or two's adventure. Only in our love of wild sport and wilderness can we ever have a meeting of minds.

Through limitations of time and distance, many of us must concentrate on wildfowling in southern Britain, but the greatest haunts of marshmen are in the far north, where the raw sea sparkles in the eye of the wild goose. Some geese venture south according to weather and food supplies, but they are like long-lost souls, wandering about making the best of our agriculture, and they do not provide the same adventure as when they are up in those wild winds above loch and mountain.

Not surprisingly, goose fever grips many southerners and they are quite prepared to make the long trip north every year to renew the ancient acquaintance. It is as if the spirit of the hunter is embodied in that bird and man must make his traditional pilgrimage to check that all is well. Once we went as predators, following the migratory flocks in due season, but now the bag is irrelevant for most men and only a minority still harbour the greed which brings the whole sport into disrepute. As long as we can make a small, reasonable cull according to each species' status and have a good day's sport we are completely satisfied.

The east coast too is steeped in wildfowling lore, for there is a happy association with the sea which stretches back into the mists of time. Like the fish of the sea, the fowl of Norfolk, Suffolk, and Essex have provided a living for many generations of hardy folk. Now the quarry list is greatly reduced and sport is the prime motivator, but how important this last link with wilderness is for twentieth-century man.

Most of the British coast is under the watchful eyes of local wildfowling clubs and together they offer some of the most underrated and challenging sport in the kingdom. If you feel this is for you, and you have the necessary stamina, then why not contact the BASC for a local contact?

# SHOOTING AND CONSERVATION –
## TOWARDS 2000

From a purely practical point of view, it is in the sporting Gun's interest to maintain or encourage healthy populations of quarry species, so that there is a shootable surplus. But the great British tradition of the sporting naturalist goes way beyond that ambition and there is no doubt that shooting's contribution to conservation continues to be substantial. Sportsmen care deeply about our countryside and coastline and all the wildlife encountered there—and not just the quarry species—and frequently commit themselves to the vital tasks of creation, or preservation and improvement, of habitat.

The gameshooter has long been in the forefront of the conservation movement. Hundreds of thousands of acres of game preserves act as protected habitat for a very wide variety of species, ranging from orchids and nightingales in and about pheasant coverts to rare merlins on grouse moors. In many cases the density of otherwise scarce animals and plants is greatly increased by sporting management, for example of butterflies and flowers in woodland rides cut specially for feeding pheasants and standing Guns in. And many scarce plants and waders thrive on marshes and in boggy corners retained primarily for duck and snipe. Without the sporting interest, much of this natural heritage would have been lost to hitherto uncompromising, profit-motivated agriculture and forestry, or to other, perhaps even more harmful, development.

All the best long-standing gameshoots have concentrated on the improvement of habitat rather than rearing and release schemes and this would seem to be the way of the future. Today big bags are both unfashionable and unwise and presentation of smaller numbers of testing birds is increasingly popular. Thus it is no longer so necessary to over-populate land with droves of hand-reared and released birds which could not exist in the wild without extensive feeding and molly-coddling by man. However, there are more and more shooters to cater for, including city folk who have little knowledge of country customs, and there is often a lowering of standards where commercialism creeps in, with embarrassingly low birds sent over.

To release birds onto land which is unfit to receive them is both a waste of time and a squandering of precious resources. In addition, the hostile environment of an estate which makes no concession to wildlife is no pleasure to sport in.

Of course, effective conservation costs money, whether in terms of direct labour and materials or indirectly through manipulation of cropping regimes, and in this the sporting interest has been invaluable. Some rich owners have always reserved land entirely for sport, but without the very considerable income from sporting lets many others would have been forced to opt for land uses which

Shooting farmers are generally more aware of the need to restrict the use of chemicals on the land, spraying only when absolutely necessary and choosing the time with great care so that the effect on bees and other wildlife is minimal. Some have learnt how selective spraying of headlands can, for example, bring a welcome increase in plant, small mammal, and butterfly populations as well as in insect food for partridges, without significant decrease in crop yields.

In all forms of quarry shooting the sportsman is in a unique position to help researchers with studies such as the wing surveys organized by the BASC. These provide a wealth of information not usually available through observation alone and not only provide for better management of quarry populations but also help to monitor trends and yield the essential statistics which are so vital in countering the distortion and misinterpretation sometimes advanced by frustrated antis.

Even in gameshooting there is much to learn and it is vital that we back, through membership at least, the Game Conservancy, whose biologists carry out important research into, for example, ways to arrest grouse population decline. They often work in conjunction with conservation and bird study organizations, who we can help through the return of rings from bagged migratory quarry. It is always fascinating to learn just how far that duck or goose has travelled.

The importance of such co-operation cannot be over-emphasized in a country where an increasingly mobile and leisure-orientated population competes for a greater stake in the outdoors. Our wildlife and landscape are treasures over which no one section of society has absolute dominion and if shooting is to continue to grow at its present rate then the modern shooter must build substantially on the already great British tradition of the sporting naturalist. He must acknowledge the fluctuating fortunes of quarry populations, be prepared for reasonable compromise, and unite with specialist conservation bodies in the major battle against habitat destruction.

Sorting the grouse bag: gameshooters can provide researchers with quarry statistics not available through observation alone.

# APPENDICES

✂

## BRITISH SHOOTING SEASONS

(All dates inclusive. Individual areas may have local restrictions. Separate seasons apply to the Irish Republic.)

*Pheasant:* 1 Oct–1 Feb (in Northern Ireland cocks only may be shot 1 Oct–31 Jan, but a licence to shoot hens may be obtained from the DoE (Conservation Branch), Stormont Castle if the applicant can provide evidence of releasing birds).

*Grey partridge:* 1 Sept–1 Feb (in Northern Ireland the season varies from year to year and is generally much shorter).

*Redlegged partridge:* 1 Sept–1 Feb (in Northern Ireland–1 Oct–31 Jan).

*Red grouse:* 12 Aug–10 Dec. (Northern Ireland 12 Aug–30 Nov.)

*Black grouse:* 20 Aug–10 Dec.

*Ptarmigan:* 12 Aug–10 Dec.

*Capercaillie:* 1 Oct–31 Jan.

*Common snipe:* 12 Aug–31 Jan (Northern Ireland 1 Sept–31 Jan).

*Jack snipe:* Northern Ireland only (1 Sept–31 Jan).

*Woodcock:* 1 Oct–31 Jan (Scotland 1 Sept–31 Jan).

*Curlew:* Northern Ireland only (1 Sept–31 Jan).

*Golden plover:* 1 Sept–31 Jan.

*Geese (pinkfooted, greylag, whitefronted, Canada):* 1 Sept-20 Feb in or over any area below High Water Mark of ordinary spring tides (basically the foreshore); 1 Sept-31 Jan elsewhere (inland) except that the whitefront may be shot in England and Wales only and in Northern Ireland all goose shooting ends on 31 Jan.

*Duck (mallard, wigeon, teal, pintail, common pochard, tufted, shoveler, gadwall, goldeneye):* 1 Sept–20 Feb in or over any area below High Water Mark of ordinary spring tides; 1 Sept–31 Jan elsewhere except that in Northern Ireland all duck shooting ends on 31 Jan.

*Coot:* 1 Sept–31 Jan (fully protected in Northern Ireland).

*Moorhen:* 1 Sept–31 Jan (fully protected in Northern Ireland).

*Woodpigeon:* can be shot at all times.

*Collared dove:* can be shot at all times except in Northern Ireland where it may only be killed or taken using poisonous or stupefying bait under licence from the DoE (Conservation Branch).

*Magpie, jay, rook, crow, jackdaw:* can be shot at all times.

*Hare:* No close season in England, Scotland, and Wales but on moorlands and unenclosed non-arable lands may be shot only by the occupier and persons authorized by him between 11 Dec and 31 Mar

(Scotland 1 Jul–31 Mar). In Northern Ireland may be shot only from 1 Oct–31 Jan unless a licence is obtained from the DoE on production of evidence that hares have been causing damage.
*Rabbit:* can be shot at all times.

☐ In England and Wales it is illegal to shoot game species (as defined by law—see page 34) on Sundays or Christmas Day.

☐ In Scotland there is no law against the shooting of quarry species on Sundays but there is an unwritten law or custom that no shooting should take place before noon on Sundays in order to prevent the disturbance of church services.

☐ In Northern Ireland it is illegal to shoot any quarry on Sundays.

☐ In England and Wales it is illegal to shoot on Sunday in Anglesey, Brecknock, Caernarvon, Cardigan, Carmarthen, Cornwall, Denbigh, Devon, Doncaster, Glamorgan, Great Yarmouth, Isle of Eley, Leeds, Merioneth, Norfolk, Pembroke, Somerset, Yorkshire (North and West Ridings).

☐ In Northern Ireland it is illegal to shoot from one hour after sunset to one hour before sunrise.

Under Section 2(6) and (7) of the Wildlife and Countryside Act 1981, the Secretary of State (Scotland is treated separately from England/Wales) has the power to declare any period not exceeding fourteen days as one of special protection for any birds listed in Part I of Schedule 2 with respect to the whole or any specified part of Great Britain. The species covered are: mallard, teal, wigeon, pintail, tufted duck, pochard, shoveler, gadwall, goldeneye, pinkfooted goose, greylag goose, whitefronted goose, Canada goose, golden plover, woodcock, snipe, coot, and moorhen.

When seven days of frozen or snow-covered ground have been so recorded in Scotland or England/Wales or both, the Nature Conservancy Council informs the BASC accordingly. If the severe weather looks likely to continue, the BASC informs secretaries of its wildfowling and gameshooting clubs, Joint Councils, and syndicates, that, if the severe weather continues for a further seven days and looks likely to continue an Order suspending the shooting of the above-mentioned species in the appropriate country is likely to be signed on the thirteenth day to take effect on the fifteenth day. The BASC also calls on the shooting community to exercise voluntary restraint where appropriate.

Should the conditions which necessitated the call for restraint continue until the thirteenth day and look likely to continue, the NCC, having consulted with the BASC and other conservation bodies, advises the appropriate Secretary of State to sign a suspension Order which would come into effect at 9 a.m. on the fifteenth day. Before signing, the Secretary of State normally consults with the BASC.

An Order is reviewed after a maximum of seven days.

## SALE OF QUARRY

☐ Game may be sold only during and up to ten days after the end of the shooting season.

☐ To sell game, a gamedealer's licence must be obtained from a Post Office unless you are selling to a licensed gamedealer, in which case an ordinary gameshooting licence is sufficient. A shoot may not sell gamebirds to its members without a gamedealer's licence.

☐ In Northern Ireland it is illegal to sell or purchase for consumption partridges and grouse, and female pheasants can only be sold or purchased for consumption if a DoE exemption to kill them has been obtained.

☐ It is illegal to sell wild geese at all times.

☐ The woodpigeon and feral pigeon may be sold dead at all times without any licence.

☐ In England, Scotland and Wales no licence is needed to sell quarry species of duck.

☐ Capercaillie, coot, tufted duck, mallard, wigeon, teal, pintail, golden plover, pochard, shoveler, common snipe, and woodcock may be sold dead from 1 Sept to 28 Feb in England, Scotland and Wales, but in Northern Ireland it is illegal to sell any wildfowl.

☐ Hares may not be sold or offered for sale during the months of March to July inclusive.

## MAJOR ORGANIZATIONS AND ADDRESSES

*The British Association for Shooting and Conservation (BASC)*
(Marford Mill, Rossett, Wrexham, Clwyd LL12 0HL; telephone 0244-570881: Scottish Office—Catter House, Drymen, Glasgow; telephone 0360-60840)

*The Game Conservancy*
(Burgate Manor, Fordingbridge, Hants SP6 1EF; telephone 0425-52381)

*The British Field Sports Society*
(59 Kennington Road, London SE1 7PZ; telephone 01-928-4742)

*The Ulster Game and Wildfowl Society*
(Hon Sec G.H. McLoud, 49 Ashdale Crescent, Bangor, Co Down; telephone 0247-469508)

*The British Shooting Sports Council*
(Secretary Mr P. A. Gouldsbury, Pentridge, Salisbury, Wilts SP5 5QX; telephone 07255-370)

*The Clay Pigeon Shooting Association (England)*
(107 Epping New Road, Buckhurst Hill, Essex IG9 5TQ; telephone 01-505-6221)

*The Ulster Clay Pigeon Shooting Association*
(Secretary S. Winston Johnston, 6 Springhill Avenue, Bangor, Co Down)

*The Scottish Clay Pigeon Shooting Association*
(Secretary Mr S. Shiach, 2 Greengill, Gilcrux, Aspatria, Carlisle, Cumbria)

*The Welsh Clay Target Shooting Association*
(Secretary Mr J. Osborne, Arbroath, 45 Picton Road, Hakin, Milford Haven, Dyfed; telephone 06462-3076)

*Isle of Man Clay Pigeon Shooting Association*
(A. D. Brew, Ballawanton Farm, The Lhen, Andreas, IOM)

*Country Landowners Association*
(16 Belgrave Square, London SW1X 8PQ; telephone 01-235-0511)

*The Game Farmers Association*
(Hon Sec S. H. Jervis-Read, The Cottage, Little Chart, near Ashford, Kent; telephone 023-384-610)

*The Birmingham Gun Barrel Proof House*
(Proof Master Mr A. G. Scott, Banbury St, Birmingham 5; telephone 021-643-3860)

*The London Gun Barrel Proof House*
(The Gunmakers Company, 48 Commercial Road, London E1)

*The Shooting Sports Trust*
(Secretary Norman Haseldine, 115 Psalter Lane, Sheffield S11 8YR; telephone 0742-585974)

*The Gun Trade Association*
(Secretary Nigel Brown, Fairbourne Cottage, Bunny Lane, Timsbury, near Romsey, Hants SO5 0PG; telephone 0794-68443)

## SPECIALIST READING

Barnes, M. and Reynolds, M., *Shooting Made Easy* (Crowood Press)
Begbie, E., *Fowler in the Wild* (David & Charles)
Boothroyd, G. *Gun Collecting* (Sportsman's Press)
Carlisle, G. *Grouse and Gun* (Stanley Paul)
Coats, A., *Pigeon Shooting* (Vista Books)
Coles, C., (Ed), *Shooting and Stalking* (Stanley Paul)
Coles, C. *Complete Guide to Game Management* (Barrie & Jenkins)
Garwood, G. T., *Shotguns and Cartridges*, (A. & C. Black)
Gray, N., *Woodland Management for Pheasants and Wildlife* (David & Charles)
Heath, V., *A Dog at Heel* (Boydell)

Humphreys, J., *Shooting Pigeons* (David & Charles)

Martin, B. P., *Sporting Birds of the British Isles* (David & Charles)

Martin, B. P., *The Great Shoots—Britain's Premier Sporting Estates* (David & Charles)

McCall, I., *Your Shoot—Gamekeeping and Management* (A. & C. Black)

McKelvie, C., *The Book of the Woodcock* (Debrett)

Mills, D. and Barnes, M., *Amateur Gunsmithing* (Boydell)

Moxon, P. R. A., *Gundogs: Training and Field Trials* (Popular Dogs Publishing)

Page, R., *The Fox and the Orchid* (fieldsports and conservation) (Quiller)

Parkes, C. and Thornley, J., *Fair Game* (shooting law) (Pelham)

Petrie-Hay, L., *Gundogs: their History, Breeding and Training* (Sportsman's Press)

Potts, G. R., *The Partridge* (Collins)

Sandys-Winch, G., *Gun Law* (Shaw & Sons)

## MAGAZINES WHICH REGULARLY FEATURE QUARRY SHOOTING

*Shooting Times and Country Magazine* (weekly), 10 Sheet St, Windsor, Berks SL4 1BG (telephone 0753-856061). The official weekly journal of the BASC. Established 1882.

*Shooting Magazine* (monthly), 10 Sheet St, Windsor, Berks SL4 1BG (telephone 0753-856061).

*Sporting Gun* (monthly), Bretton Court, Bretton, Peterborough PE3 8DZ (telephone 0733-264666).

*The Shooting Life* (monthly), Hill House, Heckfield, near Basingstoke, Hants RG27 0JY (telephone 0734-326668).

*Shooting News* (weekly), Unit 21, Plymouth Road, Industrial Site, Tavistock, Devon PL19 9QN (telephone 0822-66460).

*Insight* (quarterly), 45 Eastgate, Bourne, Lincs PE10 9JY (telephone 0778-421532).

*The Field* (monthly), Carmelite House, Carmelite Street, London EC4Y 0JA (telephone 01-353-6000).

*Countrysport* (monthly), Westley Green Farm, Valley End, Chobham, Surrey GU24 8TB (telephone 09905-6056).

*Dog and Country* (quarterly), Corry's Roestock Lane, Colney Heath, Herts AL4 0QW (telephone 0727-22614).

*Guns Review* (monthly), Broad Stone, Hepstonstell, Hebden Bridge, West Yorkshire HX7 7PH (telephone 0422-844387).

# INDEX

171

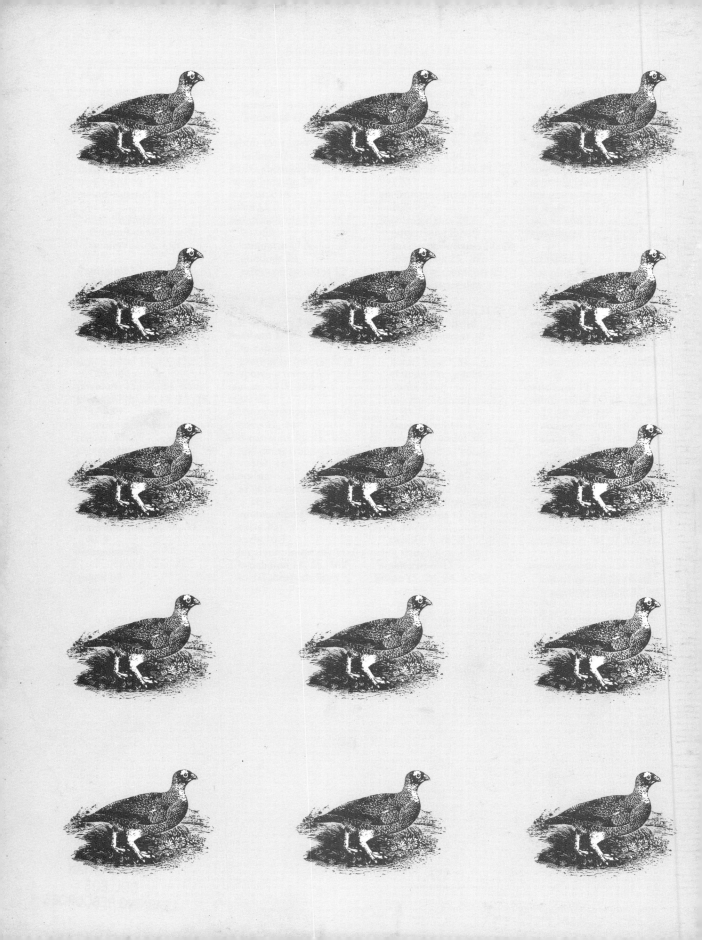